Social Thinking® and Me

Thinksheets for Social Emotional Learning
Book 2

By

Linda K. Murphy and Michelle Garcia Winner

INTERNATIONAL BOOK AWARDS FINALIST
IntlBookAwards.com

MOM'S CHOICE AWARDS
HONORING EXCELLENCE

! Social Thinking jr.®

Social Thinking Publishing, Santa Clara, California
www.socialthinking.com

Social Thinking® and Me

Thinksheets for Social Emotional Learning

Linda K. Murphy and Michelle Garcia Winner

Illustrations by NewWay Solutions, Santa Fe, Argentina

ISBN: 978-1-936943-38-8

Think Social Publishing, Inc.
404 Saratoga Avenue, Suite 200
Santa Clara, CA 95050
Tel: (408) 557-8595
Fax: (408) 557-8594

This book was printed and bound in the United States by Mighty Color Printing.

TSP is a sole source provider of Social Thinking products in the U.S.
Books may be purchased online at www.socialthinking.com

Dedications

To my mom, Jane B. Murphy, the first person who taught me how to think about others.

—Linda K. Murphy

To the parents and professionals who seek to take abstract social concepts and teach them concretely to promote a better understanding of social relationships in us all.

—Michelle Garcia Winner

Acknowledgments

I'd like to thank all the students and families that I've worked with over the years. They're the inspiration for this set of books. They continuously challenge me to be a better communicator, to stretch my thinking, to be creative, and to be flexible in my teaching. Some of my best ideas have evolved directly from conversations with my students and their parents. I'm constantly reminded that one of the most important aspects of teaching is listening.

I'd like to express my sincere gratitude to the amazing team at Think Social Publishing, Inc. Michelle Garcia Winner's passion, innovation, and common-sense thinking consistently lead our field in the right direction. Thank you to Dr. Pamela Crooke for guiding us in the process of gathering research to support our work. I give a heartfelt thanks to Veronica Zysk, who has been a wonderful mentor to me. I'd also like to thank my editor, Sandy Horwich for her valuable review of my work.

I'm extremely grateful to my dedicated team at Peer Projects Therapy from the Heart. Without each of you, your talents, and your hearts, we couldn't do the work that we do. Most importantly, I'd like to thank my loving family: Rob, Freddie, Desmond, and my father, Paul.

—Linda K. Murphy

I'd like to thank Linda Murphy for inspiring the creation of *Social Thinking and Me*. She's been incredibly flexible during its development. Our goal has been to create age-appropriate lessons students can use to help them develop improved self-regulation and better social skills that will last a lifetime.

Many thanks go to Veronica Zysk for her ongoing collaboration and her efforts to help make our teachings come to life through her copious editing and project management skills, as well as her simple human endurance. It is amazing how long each and every project takes to develop from a kernel of an idea into a finished product.

Thanks are also in order to Sandy Horwich for her editing help, and for her and Pam Crooke for their active assistance with developing the plan for the artwork and securing the art from our talented artists in Argentina, NewWaySolutions. Their art brings this project to life.

Finally, my thanks go to the many kids I've worked with over the years, kids who are in that in-between age: not quite little kids and not quite big kids. They have been my best teachers when it comes to studying human psycho-social development and have taught me they need their own special way to learn these abstract but important concepts!

—Michelle Garcia Winner

Recommended Teaching & Learning Pathway
for using **Social Thinking and Me**

Pathway for ages 8-11

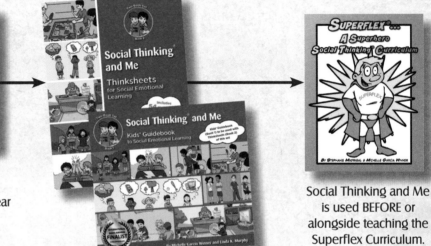

Use Social Detective first to introduce Social Thinking concepts / Vocabulary that appear in Social Thinking and Me.

Social Thinking and Me is used BEFORE or alongside teaching the Superflex Curriculum.

Pathway for ages 9-13

Use Social Thinking and Me to introduce core social concepts BEFORE using books for adolescents, such as Social Fortune or Social Fate.

Find these and other books and teaching materials at
www.SocialThinking.com

Contents

USB Drive Contents:

All Thinksheets (organized by chapter)

Letter to Parents/Caregivers

Glossary

Preface

I was very excited when Linda Murphy approached the Social Thinking team with the idea of publishing a book geared to older elementary and middle school age students so they could learn about key Social Thinking Vocabulary and concepts. Having a common language to talk about social issues is an essential component in teaching the broader Social Thinking Methodology. This is also a time in a child's social development when confusion can arise as social expectations increase while peer understanding and forgiveness of our students' struggles seems to decrease.

As we brainstormed how the book would unfold, we eventually decided to break the information into two parts: a book written in more kid-friendly language that would make Social Thinking concepts come to life for our students, coupled with a book of thinksheets to help adults guide children in learning about and practicing the concepts. We wanted this to be a tool parents and teachers could easily and effectively use with their students even if those parents and professionals didn't have prior experience teaching Social Thinking concepts. The goal in all our teaching is to promote social emotional learning that results in improved self-awareness, self-regulation, social problem solving, and empathic communication.

I was also eager to develop this material to be used as a first step in preparing upper elementary and middle school students to learn about our Superflex superhero Social Thinking curriculum. For Superflex to truly "make sense" to our students, they need to have a good grasp of the Social Thinking Vocabulary and ideas.

I've enjoyed working with Linda on this project. We hope that together we've created teaching and learning tools that will be helpful to all students and will provide parents and professionals with better methods for teaching key social concepts that form the foundation to success throughout life. In the second part of this preface, Linda discusses her background and how she developed the original idea for a book. I hope you find it as interesting as we did and incorporate this set into your toolbag for teaching students with social learning challenges.

—Michelle Garcia Winner

I began my career as a speech language pathologist over 15 years ago in early intervention in Cambridge, Massachusetts, where services were delivered in a family-centered way. This meant most sessions took place in a family's home, and parents were usually partners in my sessions. As we played together on the floor with their child, I learned early on the importance of communicating with families, listening to their concerns, and collaborating about how to best meet a child's needs.

Over time, I began a private practice. Because of the nature of the work and the growing ages of the children, parents' direct involvement in our sessions decreased. It remained important to me to find effective ways to share with parents what I was teaching during our sessions while also continuing to listen to their needs and observations of their children in other environments.

In 2005 in San Diego, I heard Michelle Garcia Winner speak about the ideas of Social Thinking for the first time. I'd just started running a social pragmatics group for young children at Emerson College in Boston and was excited to have this new resource and way of thinking. Everything about Social Thinking made so much sense to me! It invited me to shift my teaching strategies away from that of prompting specific social skills such as "saying hello" or "answering a question" to one of helping kids think about others and therefore think about why they might do something. Instead of telling kids what to do in a certain situation or moment, we could instead introduce the context as a whole in terms of what most people might expect us to do. We could also share how others might feel based on what we do and acknowledge that sometimes it can be very hard to figure all this out on our own.

Social Thinking also gave a concrete way to talk about problems and our feelings associated with these problems. It invited me to not simply try and stop a child from having a tantrum or big reaction to a disappointment but to give children vocabulary to express their feelings and help them understand how others might view that problem. They would subsequently feel empowered as they assess difficult moments on their own. I immediately purchased one of their core books, *Thinking About YOU Thinking About ME*, and then started working with Michelle's *Think Social!* curriculum as soon as it became available. I was passionate about incorporating Social Thinking ideas into my teaching and sharing these ideas with others.

As I strove to teach children Social Thinking ideas, such as expected/unexpected behavior, body and brain in the group, thinking with your eyes, and being a social detective, I found myself also wanting to share these concepts in a way that children could easily review them, as many times as they wanted to, after our session was over. I wanted to be able to provide something concrete that children could later read along with their parents, teachers, and other therapists, and something that would also educate others on Social Thinking and support broader use of the terms we were using.

In our group each week, we typically had a lesson on a particular social play or social skill in the form of a personalized Social Story™. We read a story that one of my graduate students or I had written using guidelines developed by Carol Gray.[1] For example, we used Social Stories to teach the ideas of sharing, turn taking, and even what to do when you receive a gift you may not like. I then shared our weekly lesson with parents, giving them a printed copy to read at home with their child.

As I became more familiar with Michelle's work, I began to write stories incorporating her Social Thinking ideas, and supported these ideas with pictures to further engage readers. Modeling these on the lessons in the *Think Social!* curriculum, I wrote with the goal of teaching these ideas in a way that was engaging to young children and easy for others to repeat, while ensuring I was providing families with the same teaching. I began to email PDF files of these stories to parents so they could both read them at home and share them with the other members of their child's team, including classroom teachers or school therapists. Over time, my stories began to spread, and they're now used in several schools in our Massachusetts area. I continue to share them so that Social Thinking Vocabulary and teachings reach as wide an audience as possible. It's well known that the more consistent everyone is with the language and concepts they use, the more effective the teaching!

A few years ago, I approached the Social Thinking team with my idea for a book to teach Social Thinking concepts to kids in upper elementary and middle school in a way that was simple enough for them to learn but not so complex that it would seem like "work." I also wanted this book to be something others could access so that parents, teachers, and therapists could use consistent language with children while teaching Social Thinking ideas. This has been important to me because I've seen many children benefit from Social Thinking Vocabulary and teaching, especially when the adults around them understand and use it as well.

---

1   For more information about Carol Gray and Social Stories, visit
    http://carolgraysocialstories.com/social-stories/

Here's an example. One student I've been working with for a few years is a talented artist. It's amazing to watch her draw with detail and care. However, it hasn't always been fun for others in the room when she makes a mistake in her work or accidentally rips her paper! Crying and meltdowns have been fairly common reactions. Recently, however, this girl was drawing a picture of a princess when I saw her paper rip. She stopped what she was doing and looked at me saying, "Linda, my paper ripped!" "I see that!," I replied and waited quietly, allowing her space to think about the situation on her own. We've had many talks over the course of our time together about problems and reaction sizes, and her parents have also carried on these discussions at home. I felt confident that she could handle the rip and waited with anticipation to see what she might say or do next. She smiled and said, "But it's just a glitch. Maybe we can tape it." Hooray! I agreed, handed her some tape, and she and a friend fixed her paper together. At the end of our session, she showed her drawing to her mother, more proud of the fixed glitch than of the actual drawing itself. Her mom and I shared the same pride. This is one very real example of a child using Social Thinking Vocabulary and concepts to help herself appraise and manage a situation that previously had been hard to bear. It's this type of increased self-awareness, improved perspective, and successful self-management that keeps me teaching Social Thinking!

From my first contact with the Social Thinking team in 2010, my ideas related to this project have evolved with their help. We changed the focus to students in upper elementary and middle school and expanded it to include chapters that provide comprehensive yet kid-friendly discussions of what a particular Social Thinking idea means. Along the way we realized that kids won't want to lug around a 300+ page book, so we broke it out into one book written for kids, and a second written more for the adults working with these individuals. The second book includes worksheets we now call "thinksheets" to give plenty of opportunities to practice the concepts being learned. It's our hope that as readers immerse themselves in each chapter, they come out with a stronger understanding of each concept, and are better able to plug these ideas into real-life social interactions.

It was a pleasure to capture moments from the Social Thinking work I do through many very real examples in the chapters and thinksheets. Through the use of Social Thinking ideas, I've seen many children grow, change, and become more aware of their own thinking and actions. I've watched them become more competent, confident, and flexible social thinkers, both in the classroom and among their peers. The Social Thinking Vocabulary and curriculum have provided an invaluable framework to guide the teaching of Social Thinking. My hope is that this set of books will offer one more way to share these important ideas and ways of thinking with others, while promoting consistency in how we respectfully talk about these things with our kids who have social challenges.

— Linda K. Murphy

WhaT is SociaL Thinking?

"How do you do?"
"Hello."
"Hi!"
"Hey."
"What sup?"
... a nod of the head, a wave of the hand, eye contact with a smile...

These are all different forms of greeting another person that range from more to less formal and that most people "learn" over time, through observation of others, and through being part of the daily flow of life. When a person's social brain development is on track, a social sense and social awareness develops as children grow and are exposed to different settings and situations. It starts with simple interactions during early childhood and matures over time and experience sharing. Yet many individuals of all ages, diagnosed with a social-emotional or social-communication disorder, such as ASD, SDC, ADHD, twice exceptional, NVLD, hyperlexia, etc., or with no diagnosis at all, have brains that don't process nor make sense of the thousands of bits of social information that surround us every day.

We don't often stop to think about how we become the social beings we are. Most adults assume social information is acquired indirectly, almost as though it's an intuitive sense we all share. Because of this assumption, even in structured teaching settings like a classroom or therapy room, adults *encourage* social information but are less likely to *teach* it in any concrete way. Adults may tell children to pay attention, respect your teacher, cooperate with your peers, get in a group, and use a host of other socially-laden concepts to direct their attention to their surroundings and how to interact with others. We just assume kids know what we mean and will respond accordingly. Paying attention, cooperating, and showing respect are huge and complex social concepts comprised of many different aspects of functioning—concepts that don't carry any value or importance for kids who don't intuitively know what they mean.

1

"Social thinking" is the term we use to remind parents, educators, therapists, counselors, and our clients that our brains continually consider social information (whether or not we are interacting with others) and that we all engage in a lifelong social learning process. Our social learning abilities are the wellspring from which we learn how to effectively interact with others across the many situations and settings of our daily lives.

Consider the simplicity and the complexity of the following statement: **Having good social skills means *we use our social thinking to problem solve how to adapt effectively based on the situation and the people in the situation.***

It reminds us that our social skills are not behaviors that are simply rehearsed, memorized, and produced based on a singular stimulus or response. In fact, if we reflect back to the opening of this section, it can be easily argued that people who say "hi" to every person the exact same way, every time they see each other (even if that's multiple times per day), regardless of whether the person is a stranger, an acquaintance, or a favorite aunt, that person would likely be interpreted as quirky or odd by others. A 13-year-old boy who says, "How do you do" or "I am pleased to see you again" instead of the more commonly expected responses of "Hey" or "What's up?" is someone whose social awareness of people, place, and social expectations warrants further attention.

Our social behaviors, what we commonly call our social skills, are *behaviors we observe in each other that we gauge against a common set of expectations and assumptions.* Our social skills are actually part of a larger system that begins with our social thinking and unfolds through our social problem solving. These skills hinge on our accurate and rapid ability to read the situation, consider the people in the situation (their thoughts, feelings, and reactions), while simultaneously using our prior knowledge and our social brains to figure out the social-emotional expectations of us in that setting.

In reality, we use our social thinking far more often than we use our social skills. It's our social thinking that guides us throughout our day and provides the thinking tools that help us navigate through situations, stay on track with social expectations, and make decisions along the way. Yet, think about how we teach and relate to others in relation to our social abilities. In our roles as parents, teachers, or therapists our emphasis is typically on skills, on behavior. We just assume the social thinking comes along naturally, right?

Social Thinking® is a teaching methodology that avoids all these assumptions by providing individuals with concepts, a unique vocabulary, and materials that explode the social code and teach individuals to become stronger social thinkers and social problem solvers. The methodology breaks down complex social concepts into smaller concrete chunks that can be explained in a way that is meaningful for those whose social brains process information differently. When explaining how we teach about abstract social concepts, we use the following definition to better describe the larger social learning process that is at the heart of Social Thinking.

Three-Part Definition of Social Thinking

1 First engage in Social Thinking
Social thinking is the ability to consider our own and others' thoughts, emotions, beliefs, intentions, knowledge, etc., and think about all this within the context of the situation. This "mental data gathering" helps us interpret the situation and figure out how to respond (or not respond) through our social behaviors (which includes language). Social thinking relates to our ability to take perspective, our own and that of others, while tapping into our executive functioning abilities. These abilities help us figure out our social goals and construct our social behavioral plans. They also are important factors in narrative language, reading comprehension, and written expression. Our social thinking is our "meaning maker" that helps us make sense of the facts and information we are learning.

2 Next comes social skills

Based on our social thoughts and the social data we gather, we then adapt our social behaviors based on the situation and what we know (or don't know) about the people in the situation. The goal is to effectively interpret the situation to produce acceptable (we call them "expected") social skills to increase the likelihood that people will respond to us in the manner we had hoped.

3 Finally, consider the desired emotional response we want in others

Our social skills are interpreted and responded to by others first at the emotional level and then at the intellectual level. Feelings hit first; then we get our brains involved. People form judgments about us and our behaviors that largely arise from these emotional reactions. If we feel good, or at least okay, in response to something a person does or says, we tend to think that person has good social skills, and we may describe him or her in a positive or favorable way. If we feel uncomfortable in response to something a person does or says, we tend to think that person has weak or poor social skills. We may describe the person as awkward, rude, odd, quirky, or impolite. How people emotionally respond to our social behaviors often leads to how they treat us in return. If we feel good during an interaction, we may smile or engage more. If we feel disturbed or annoyed or even slightly uncomfortable, we may turn away or react in a negative way.

Our social behaviors influence how people feel about us and how they react to us. In turn, this affects how we feel about them, and possibly, ourselves. It's a constant dance of thoughts, feelings, and behaviors going back and forth. To be effective social partners, we are continually reading the situation and adjusting our social skills accordingly. As a teaching methodology, Social Thinking helps individuals understand the many aspects of social interaction and being part of a group and provides concrete curricula, tools, strategies, and materials to help individuals think socially and problem solve at a social level.

Social Thinking concepts and materials are based on research that explores the social emotional development of all students as well as research completed in the fields of ASD, ADHD, and other social learning disorders. The ideas and strategies taught in *Social Thinking and Me* address research-based concepts that are at the foundation of social emotional learning, social relatedness, and conceptual understanding: theory of mind, central coherence theory, and executive functioning. A team of researchers at the University of Arizona studied the effectiveness of teaching Social Thinking Vocabulary to promote the generalization of social skills across settings. The 2008 study by Crooke, Hendrix, and Rachman, "Brief Report: Measuring the Effectiveness of Teaching Social Thinking to Children with Asperger Syndrome (AS) and High Functioning Autism (HFA)" was published in the *Journal of Autism and Developmental Disorders*.

The Social Thinking® Vocabulary: What It Is and Why It's Important

Social Thinking is a language-based teaching methodology comprised of concepts, frameworks, and materials that explain social concepts in a different, more concrete way. This helps people notice more clearly what is happening around them as they socially relate to others. At the heart of the methodology is the Social Thinking Vocabulary (STV). Terms and concepts such as "think with your eyes," "body, eyes, ears, and brain in the group," "hidden rules," or "expected/unexpected behavior" give more explicit direction to individuals as they learn about their social thinking. This unique language helps individuals notice the social expectations of the setting so they can then use thinking strategies to develop stronger social self-awareness and social problem solving skills.

The goal in creating the vocabulary is to give professionals, parents, and kids of all types a common language they can use across their childhood and into adulthood, a language that will guide them toward a deeper understanding of the many moving parts that go into developing and maintaining social relationships and working as part of a group. The importance of this shared language can't be emphasized strongly enough. Children and adults who struggle in the areas of social-emotional learning and social communication need a different way to learn about social constructs that are abstract, complicated, and complex. As mentioned earlier, teaching discrete social behaviors is an ineffective way of helping these individuals do better in social situations. Despite their often strong abilities in academics and factual thinking, these individuals are often noticeably weak in their social processing; they need concrete help. Through teaching the vocabulary, both adults and children are learning concepts they can use across all parts of the day and in all settings, from the classroom to the dinner table to the grocery store. The usefulness of the concepts and vocabulary extend long after these books are finished and the material is taught. They are lifelong tools that help individuals in their social thinking and social problem solving, no matter what situation they encounter.

Using *Social Thinking and Me* to Teach Social Emotional Concepts

Social Thinking and Me is a two-book set that guides adults in teaching core Social Thinking Vocabulary and social-emotional concepts to children ages 9-13. Book 1, *Social Thinking Kids' Guidebook*, speaks directly to kids and their learning level. It contains 11 chapters written in kid-friendly language that each address a single vocabulary concept. The concepts build upon each other from chapter to chapter as children start with simpler ideas that expand outward in complexity.

Book 2, *Social Thinking Thinksheets*, is designed for parents and professionals and contains 54 "thinksheets" that give kids lots of practice in using the concepts and learning them at a deeper level. The thinksheets encourage kids to do their own thinking around the vocabulary they are learning while comparing that thinking to others in their classroom or treatment group.

Book 2 also contains helpful tips directed to adults who will be teaching the Social Thinking Vocabulary, a glossary of the terms (also included in the kids' book), a letter to parents about Social Thinking, as well as extension activities for each concept that expand the teaching beyond the pages of the books.

The two books dovetail each other: Chapter 1 in the *Kids' Guidebook* has its corresponding chapter in the *Thinksheets* book, both exploring the same concept in different ways. Why two books? Honestly, the original plan was just one book. But we found we had so much good information to share we didn't want to overwhelm our readers, both kids *and* adults! While the *Kids' Guidebook* is written mainly for kids, both books in the set are meant to be used with adult guidance. A lot of conversation happens when teaching social concepts to our kids!

Social Thinking and Me is also an excellent teaching companion to use with kids in upper elementary school who are using our curriculum: *Superflex®... A Superhero Social Thinking® Curriculum* (Madrigal and Winner, 2008). The more children learn to conceptualize and use different Social Thinking concepts, vocabulary, and strategies to adapt their behaviors, the more effectively their own Superflex is able to defeat their Unthinkables.

What Are "Thinksheets"?

You may be wondering why we're using "thinksheets" instead of "worksheets" in talking about the hands-on exercises we created to support the teaching we're doing? Over the years we've found that most adults working with kids in a teaching role (parents, therapists, educators) put worksheets in front of kids and walk away. They seem to view them as "independent study" for kids to do on their own.

That's just not how we teach Social Thinking. Thinksheets are like "mini-lesson plans" and our goal in using them is to foster our students' ability to cognitively consider the social world and their experiences in it. Given this is all within the realm of "social," we then encourage kids to share their thinking with each other and learn from each other. The conversations that ensue are building pivotal skills in our kids. They are learning to take the point of view of others (perspective taking), learning to be more flexible in their own thinking and behaviors, and realizing that thoughts are connected to feelings, which are connected to reactions and responses that all contribute to the way we work together or spend time together as a group.

If we once again return to the common way social skills are taught, with a "right way" and a "wrong way" in a particular situation, we can begin to understand that teaching at the thinking level takes us on an entirely different journey. We're working most of the time in the "shades of gray" of social behaviors that are context and people dependent. People's thoughts and feelings have huge variations and so do their interpretations and perspectives. Social Thinking is all about flexible thinking and encouraging that type of flexibility in thoughts, words, and actions as a core part of the teaching.

The Social-Academic Connection

The Social Thinking Methodology includes curricula and materials that partner well in IEP development, PBIS (Positive Behavioral Interventions and Supports), SEL (social and emotional learning), and RTI (Response to Intervention) initiatives. Core Social Thinking teaching frameworks, concepts, and strategies are adaptable to individuals of all ages. They provide the link that connects our students' thinking to their own personal self-monitoring and self-regulation systems. As students become increasingly mindful of their social surroundings and how their own behavior impacts others, this awareness fosters improved self-regulation and self-control.

As we begin to deconstruct the social mind and the social learning process, it becomes more and more apparent that our social mind not only fuels our ability to adapt our social skills more effectively, it also helps us interpret and respond to academic lessons that require us to consider others' thoughts, feelings, intentions, beliefs, motives, plans, etc.

As a matter of fact, social learning and social thinking are embedded in the Common Core and State Standards of Education by which our educators teach students. These standards require students to demonstrate point of view, describe, compare, or contrast information about how characters are thinking and feeling, and use context-sensitive vocabulary in doing so. This all taps heavily into one's social understanding of the world. The English Language Arts Standards apply to reading, writing, speaking, and listening, all areas where social understanding is a major player in understanding what is being taught and what learning students are expected to demonstrate. Many of the standards involve critical thinking, problem solving, and using executive functioning skills to be successful.

The social mind is the bridge that helps us connect our own thinking and experiences to those of others. Historically in our teaching programs we have taken social cognition for granted. Mainstream teachers typically expect students to come into the classroom with a solid functioning social mind that students can use in working through curriculum lessons across a wide range of subjects. Teachers are not well-equipped to teach students who come to school with limited perspective-taking skills how to figure out the social thoughts, feelings, and intentions of the characters or subjects they are studying. The expectation is students can do this on their own.

Using Social Thinking materials, students not only learn how to think about others as a pathway to their own improved social and self-regulation skills, they also use this same social knowledge to interpret and respond to academic curriculum. The materials and tools of Social Thinking help our students develop and become stronger in the five pivotal core competencies that are at the heart of social and emotional learning (SEL): self-awareness, self-management, social awareness, relationship skills, and responsible decision-making. These skills are the foundation learning needed for Common Core and State Standards of education. Academics and Social Thinking are inextricably intertwined.

Who Is This Book For?

Social Thinking and Me was created for use in the mainstream, with children in upper elementary or middle (or junior high) school as a social-emotional curriculum to benefit *all* students, not just those with social-emotional learning challenges. Kids with intact social abilities still benefit from learning the Social Thinking Vocabulary and the thinking strategies offered in this two-book set. We are social learners at all ages and stages of our lives and these materials increase awareness of our social thinking and related social skills. Many elementary and middle school classroom educators have embraced teaching Social Thinking to all students in their classrooms. Some principals around the country have adopted these teachings for every student in the school.

This same material can be used in tandem with our broader set of materials that are tailored to those who need higher levels of RTI and/or individualized or small group specialized treatment. Social Thinking's materials in general are to be used with students who have solid to strong language and academic learning skills. These students may have no diagnosis or may be diagnosed as ASD, ADHD, twice-exceptional, hyperlexia, or with social behavior or social communication disorders. Perspective-taking skills may be emerging or established, and the child is able to engage in reasoning and problem-solving discussions at an emerging or a more developed level. Other children who will benefit greatly from this teaching material are those who have strong language and reasoning skills yet in natural environments demonstrate social challenges related to impulsivity, attention, anxiety, or self-regulation.

Teachers are also finding that children today are spending more time face-to-face with their computers, tablets, or cellphones, and less time face-to-face with their peers in real-time social interactions. As a result, teachers are noticing a decline in students' social awareness and social interaction skills. The concepts and thinksheets in *Social Thinking and Me* help foster better social awareness and develop a broader understanding of how to share space effectively, work in a group, and get along with others in both academic and social situations. This, in turn, fosters the growth of interpersonal skills, including classroom collaboration, peer friendships, and networking skills.

An off-shoot benefit of *Social Thinking and Me* is the mentoring opportunities it facilitates. You'll find that peers in the classroom will learn this vocabulary and enjoy using it across settings as well. As they do, encourage them to use the language to coach students whose brains find social learning to be more difficult. For example, if a student is wandering around the room and not working well with others, a peer mentor could say: "I'm having an uncomfortable thought because you're not keeping your body in the group. It would help us all if you come sit in your chair and work with us in the group." Although teachers are discouraged from pointing out the negative, students who are strong peer mentors use this language well to provide more reality-based feedback. Many of our students tell us it would be nice to know why other kids don't want to be with them and what they could do to help themselves be better social partners! However, also work with peers to notice when a student is doing expected behaviors and talk about these as well by saying things like, "Wow, nice job figuring out the size of the problem and staying calm. That makes us all feel better." This supports PBIS initiatives for creating a caring, collaborative, and supportive school culture for all students, one that accepts and embraces differences in learning.

How to Teach the Concepts and Chapters

Books 1 and 2 in this set support each other and while children can be encouraged to read the *Kids' Guidebook* on their own after initial teaching of the concepts, we recommend the thinksheets always be worked on together. Social thinking and social learning is complex and multi-layered learning. Adults provide the often-needed structure and real-life examples that keep learning alive for students.

The chapters in the *Kids' Guidebook* build on the ideas in the previous chapters, so it's best to introduce them in the order they're presented.

Please don't skip the first couple of chapters thinking they may be too simple or too general for your academically bright students; they present key concepts and set the stage for the remainder of the book.

At the beginning of each thinksheets chapter we've also included an extension activity you can do with students to reinforce what they're learning. You can use these activities as is or adapt them for your students. Some of the activities are based on lessons in Michelle's book, *Think Social! A Social Thinking® Curriculum for School-Age Students* (Winner, 2008). You can also refer to that book for other activities ideas to support teaching the Social Thinking Vocabulary.

Pacing yourself and your students

How quickly or slowly you introduce students to the Social Thinking Vocabulary and concepts depends, in large measure, on the student or the group. Kids who are typically developing in their social abilities will move through the content much more quickly. Those with social learning challenges (ASD, ADHD, NVLD, SEL, etc.) will need far more time spent on learning the concepts, discussing the examples, and making sense of how each concept relates to others, to our social experiences in general, and to their own lives specifically. Social learning is "slow and deep." Some chapters are more complex than others and while students may grasp the concepts in one chapter at one pace, you may find them struggling in others. You may spend two sessions on one chapter and its corresponding thinksheets yet need three or four (or more) sessions on another. Let your students be your guide in setting the pace as you work through the chapters and thinksheets. Chapter 2 is titled "Social Thinking = Flexible Thinking" and that concept is appropriate to keep in mind as you work through these materials with your students.

We recommend a 30–45 minute session to work on Social Thinking concepts with a child or group that contains students with social learning challenges. If you have more time, that's great! You'll find you can easily use it up, especially with our kids with social learning challenges! Not all children will fully comprehend a Social Thinking concept right away. If this happens and it seems a child's understanding is slow in coming, know that this is okay. Keep working at it. If a child continues to express confusion or frustration around the topics presented in the book, it may be possible she needs topics broken down further or presented at a slower pace or that she isn't yet ready for this book. With these children, you might try reviewing concepts during an individual teaching session rather than in a group setting.

It's critical for parents and professionals to use the core Social Thinking Vocabulary introduced in this book—as well as in other Social Thinking materials—in everyday language during teachable moments. For example, when a teacher has her students working as part of a group she can encourage them to "think with your eyes" and "keep your body, eyes, ears, and brain in the group." She can also acknowledge which students are doing this well. When students hear parents and professionals use Social Thinking concepts throughout the day, it helps them learn that they apply in a range of situations and not just to those covered in the book or while in a structured learning setting, such as a classroom or therapy session.

Overall let your goal be to introduce and discuss the social concepts and give the child or group sufficient time to learn the new information, internalize it, process what it means on an individual level, and practice using it. This also gives you ample opportunity to capitalize on real-life moments when you can apply focused Social Thinking language and ideas in a meaningful way.

How We Use Language and the Language We Use

Language is the medium through which we talk about and teach children about their social thinking and social skills. Yet, language can take many different forms, from giving commands or directives to asking questions, making comments, or sharing feelings. From a social perspective, we want to be mindful of the language we use with our children and how we use that language!

Unlike teaching math, where concepts such as 2 + 2 = 4 are factual and answers to problems are concretely right or wrong, teaching about social thinking and social problem solving requires a different approach. In expanding our children's social awareness, consider that children often learn best not when we ask them questions but when we "think out loud" and share information about our own internal thinking processes. Commenting on our observations of people and the setting, our emotions, our doubts and wonders is all part of what is called *declarative language*. (Its opposite is *imperative language*: language in the form of questions or commands that require a particular response.) This means we relate to students by sharing our thoughts, ideas, observations, and reasoning out loud, and we encourage children to share theirs in return. We mindfully narrate these things with the intention of increasing children's understanding and guiding their thinking and decision making.

In teaching Social Thinking, we are focused on teaching from a thinking perspective; our immediate goal is not a specific behavioral response and therefore the process we use with students shouldn't mainly rely on a question-response format. Using a thinking-out-loud way of communicating provides an additional avenue through which we can demonstrate how our social minds work and problem solve through situations.

Here's one example. Imagine a child is in art class and reacts to spilling a jar of red paint as if it's a big problem, and that child hasn't yet mastered the understanding of problem and reaction sizes. We wouldn't want to quiz him in that moment with questions such as, "What size is your problem? Is that a big problem? What should your reaction be?" This is because he may not know the right answer, and in that moment it likely feels like a big problem to him. Instead we want to calmly guide the child by saying something like, "Oh, you spilled the red paint! I remember that spilling something is just a glitch because we can fix it really easily. Let's clean it up together and then get another jar of paint. That would be a small reaction." When children (and adults too!) are upset, they cannot easily think or access what they know or are learning. Sometimes that results in the person feeling anxious on top of already feeling upset. This style of speaking can also be used to reassure the child while guiding him or her in how to manage and problem solve the social situation.

Words allow us to share what may have otherwise gone unnoticed or un-appreciated, whether it's a social action, a thought or feeling, or a reaction or response. Mindfully using our language and verbally illuminating our thought processes require us all (kids *and* adults) to slow down and think, become better observers of our environment and other people, and take note of those moments when a decision may need to be made. This type of intentional communication provides an ideal social framework for help-ing children learn the social concepts and social skills we are trying to teach.

Keep Learning Alive!

Social Thinking is 24/7; the concepts and Vocabulary you are teaching are valuable tools to be used across the day and in all situations you encounter with your students, clients, or children. The Family Letter at the end of this section can be used by teachers and therapists to introduce Social Thinking to students' parents or caregivers so they can extend learning at home.

As you move through the concepts in the *Kids' Guidebook* and the accompanying thinksheets, stay mindful of your language, think out loud often, and use and continually review previously learned ideas as naturally occurring moments and events occur. Remember to review and discuss these concepts during moments when the child is calm, happy, and able to engage in conversation. This is when learning is maximized.

- "Oh, Amanda has gotten up and left the table. Her body and brain aren't in the group right now — this makes me think she might not be interested in working with the other students."

- "I'm so happy to see your small reaction to that glitch of not playing the video game you chose! I bet your friends feel happy being around you because you're handling glitches well."

• "Wow! I noticed you really had a big reaction to that problem. I'm wondering though, did you think it was a big problem or was it really just a glitch? I wonder what a better reaction would have been...We'll have to remember that next time something like this happens."

Specific thoughts for parents using this book on their own

Children will benefit most if you use Social Thinking Vocabulary and language naturally with the whole family, not just the child with social challenges. For example, you might say, "Okay everyone! The group plan right now is to put on your pajamas!" or "We're almost ready to go but I want you to think with your eyes to see if you've forgotten something important." As a parent, you're also in the unique position to truly help children use their social memory to figure something out because you've seen your child in many different situations, across many different environments, over many years! "I remember last time we went to the movies, we saw what you wanted to see. I'm thinking it would be most fair to let your brother choose this time. This is a great time for you to practice flexible thinking!" Siblings can also be positive mentors in the learning process by using Social Thinking Vocabulary to provide direct feedback on expected/unexpected behavior.

Enjoy the Process

Do keep in mind that social learning is a process. As children become familiar with these concepts, changes happen, but they don't happen overnight. It takes a team effort involving parents, teachers, and therapists to notice, think about, reflect, offer practical solutions, and model flexible thinking alongside a child. When parents, teachers, and therapists understand and use Social Thinking concepts and vocabulary, children are helped with internalizing these ideas and moving toward greater social thinking independence.

Learn More About Social Thinking

Although it's not mandatory to do any pre-reading about Social Thinking before using *Social Thinking and Me* with students or clients, parents and professionals may want to first learn more about the broader concepts related to Social Thinking. The Social Thinking website (www.socialthinking.com) is the place to start, offering many different books and materials written by Michelle Garcia Winner and the Social Thinking team. The three books that follow will deepen readers' understanding of what Social Thinking is and how this teaching differs from other social skills methodologies:

- *Inside Out: What Makes a Person with Social Cognitive Deficits Tick?*

- *Thinking About YOU Thinking About ME*

- *Why Teach Social Thinking®? Questioning Our Assumptions on What It Means to Learn Social Skills*

Thinking About YOU Thinking About ME outlines the Social Thinking philosophy and is a precursor to the core teaching frameworks presented in a fourth and valuable book: *Think Social! A Social Thinking® Curriculum for School-Age Children.* This book is filled with lesson plans and activity ideas to teach Social Thinking. Select lessons from the *Think Social* curriculum are referenced in different parts of *Social Thinking and Me.*

Social Thinking offers a host of other books that teach core Social Thinking concepts to other age groups ranging from early learners to adults. Visit the products pages to find materials grouped for different ages.

In addition to these books, individuals visiting the Social Thinking website will find a wealth of other teaching/learning resources, to include free webinars, eLearning and online learning courses, and free information and articles about Social Thinking and social emotional learning. Sign up for the free monthly newsletter to learn about new articles and Social

Thinking conferences offered in locations across the U.S. and around the world. www.socialthinking.com

Ten helpful resources about...

1. Why Use the Social Thinking Methodology? 19 Concepts to Consider

2. Where Do I Start with Social Thinking?

3. The Social Communication Dance: The Four Steps of Communication

4. Social Behavior Starts with Social Thought: The Four Steps of Perspective Taking

5. The Social Thinking-Social Communication Profile™-Levels of the Social Mind

6. Research to Frameworks to Practice: Social Thinking's Layers of Evidence

7. Social Thinking's Competency Model: Attend-Interpret-Problem Solve-Respond (free webinar)

8. Updates on Social Thinking's Cascade of Social Attention: A Conceptual Framework to Explore a Systems Approach to Social-Communication

9. Social Thinking-Social Learning Tree

10. Understanding Core Social Thinking Challenges: The ILAUGH Model

Glossary

Big problem: A problem is big if it causes people we care about or ourselves to become hurt or sick. It's also big if people can't make money for a while or they lose their place to live. Some examples are an earthquake, a flood, or a tornado. Big problems are serious problems that adults handle. They're too big for children to figure out what to do. Big problems can make us feel nervous or sad. We may cry and see other people crying about big problems. (See also Medium problem and Glitch.)

Body in the group: When people turn or move their bodies to show others they want to be with each other, we describe this as their "body is in the group." This may mean we face each other when we speak or we move closer to another person. It may even mean we stay together when walking or moving to a new space. Our body is in the group when our head, eyes, shoulders, trunk, legs and feet are pointing toward the person speaking or the group and we are in close proximity to others.

Brain in the group: Keeping your brain in the group means you try to keep your thoughts focused on what other people are talking about.

Clean up: (see the Three Parts of doing an activity/hanging out)

Expected behavior: Behavior that most people do in a certain place or certain situation that follows the rules for that situation. Some of those rules may be hidden rules that people need to figure out. When people have expected behavior, others usually have good or okay thoughts about that behavior. (Read about the opposite: unexpected behavior.)

Flexible thinking: When we think in new or different ways about a situation, and when we feel okay with others thinking different things than we do.

Glitch: A small problem, a little unexpected situation that can be easily fixed as long as you stay calm. A small problem usually doesn't last too long. Glitches can involve just yourself or sometimes they involve one or a few other people too. They can usually be fixed easily, even though sometimes you may need some help to do this from your teacher or parent or even a friend.

Good thoughts/Uncomfortable thoughts: We all have thoughts about others. When another person makes us feel good, we probably have good thoughts about what that person says or does. For example, we may think, "He's nice" or "I like her." We usually have good thoughts about others when they act in an expected way for a situation. When another person makes us feel not so good, or upset, we may have uncomfortable thoughts about that person's behavior. These are some examples of uncomfortable thoughts: "I don't like when she does that." "I feel nervous because of what he's doing." "I'm upset at her for doing that." Uncomfortable thoughts usually happen when someone is using unexpected behavior.

Group: A group is more than one person sharing the same space or interacting together in a situation. A group can be as small as two people or it can be large, with many people.

Group plan: When people are together they usually are thinking about and doing the same thing. This is called the group plan. Following the group plan is different than following one's own plan.

Hidden rules: Most situations have hidden rules in them, which are the ways that people should behave in that situation that aren't said out loud or taught to us directly. People don't usually tell others the hidden rules for every situation. But, people are expected to figure them out by thinking with their eyes and listening with their ears to the people around them.

Just Me person: Someone who thinks only about himself or herself. It's okay to be a Just Me when it's a time that you can do what you want to do and it won't disrupt others.

Medium problem: Things that happen that we didn't expect and aren't easy to quickly fix. Medium problems may include fighting with another person, losing something important to you, or someone saying something really mean to another person or to you. Medium problems will make you or someone around you upset. Adults and kids usually solve medium problems together.

Nonverbal communicating: This is using your body or your gestures to send a silent message to others. For instance, you might point at something you want, or you might turn your entire body away from someone when you're mad.

Observing: Taking your time to look around at the people and the situation to find helpful clues about what's going on. Observing involves using your eyes, ears, and other senses, and thinking with your eyes.

People files: As we gather information about other people and situations, we keep that information in our brain in an imaginary set of files that we call our People Files. Everyone has their own set of people files in their brains and they can be different from person to person.

Problem: Something that happens that was not part of the plan and causes us or others around us to feel sad, nervous, upset, angry or have other negative feelings.

Reactions: Our reactions are the behaviors we show on the outside that come from the feelings we have on the inside.

Reaction size: We all have reactions to problems, and our reactions usually have feelings attached to them. It's expected behavior (and a hidden rule) that your reaction should only be as big as your problem. This means, you can have a big reaction to a big problem, a medium reaction to a medium problem, and a small reaction to a glitch. When your reaction matches the size of your problem, other people are more understanding of your behavior.

Set up: (see the Three Parts of doing an activity/hanging out)

Situation: A big word that means all the things around you. When you're using social thinking in a situation, you have to think about the *what*, the *who*, and the *where*. This means, you think about what's happening, where it's happening, and who is involved in what's happening.

Small problem: (see Glitch)

Smart guess: When you use what you already know and any clues you can find in the situation you're in, you make what's called a smart guess. (Read about the opposite: Whacky guess.)

Social detective: When people are good observers, they start to act like social detectives. That's because they're figuring out what people are thinking and feeling around them.

Social memory: This is using our brain to store all the facts and details that we've learned about people and situations. We can use our social memory to figure out what to say to others and what to do in a situation by remembering what we know about them.

Social thinking: The type of thinking your brain does about yourself and other people in relation to each other. When you use your social thinking, you think about what others are trying to do or tell you and what you can do to let people know what you want or how you feel.

Spacing out: Sometimes our brain gets tired. When we are not doing a good job thinking with our eyes and paying attention we call this being "spaced out."

Stuck thinking: Stuck on your own ideas; thinking about only one thing or thinking in only one way. This is the opposite of flexible thinking and is unexpected behavior. When you show stuck thinking, situations are more difficult and people can feel tense, frustrated, sad or mad.

Thinking and feeling: What we think always affects how we feel. Feelings are physical sensations in our bodies that seem to pop up on their own. Really, they're related to a thought we've had. Most of the time, we act in a certain way or do a certain thing because of how we're thinking or feeling.

Thinking of Others person: A Thinking of Others person means you think about how your behavior makes others think and feel. When you're a Thinking of Others person, you're always thinking about the other people who are sharing space with you or may be coming to share your space very soon. (Read about the opposite: a Just Me person.)

Thinking with your eyes: In Social Thinking we call the ability to observe and make sense of what's in front of us, thinking with your eyes. It pretty much means what it sounds like. You use your eyes to look at people and things, and then you use your brain to think about what you're seeing. This helps you figure out if you should be involved in what's going on. If you're supposed to be involved, what should you do? You think with your eyes more and figure it out!

Three Parts of doing an activity/hanging out: (1) **Set up** is getting our materials or bodies ready for a game, an activity, or just spending time with others; (2) **Doing an activity/hanging out** is the time we spend involved in the activity; (3) **Clean up** is ending the game or activity by putting away our materials or deciding together that it's time to end what we're doing.

Unexpected behavior: The opposite of expected behavior. It's behavior that most people wouldn't do in a situation and isn't expected. Unexpected behavior is when people aren't following the expected rules, hidden or stated, in the situation. When people have unexpected behavior, others usually have uncomfortable thoughts about what that person is saying or doing.

Wacky guess: This is a silly guess you make when you don't have any information about the situation and can't find any clues to help you think about what's going on.

Whopping topic change: Making comments or asking questions about things that are completely unrelated to what the group is talking about or doing. This is unexpected behavior that makes people uncomfortable.

LeTTer To ParenTs/caregivers

Date:

Dear _____,

Your child's Social Thinking® lessons will now, in part, be taught using a book called *Social Thinking and Me* by Linda K. Murphy and Michelle Garcia Winner. This product actually contains two books. Book 1 is a kids' guidebook that explains different Social Thinking concepts and introduces them in a kid-friendly way. Kids can read this book by themselves once they've gone through the content initially with an adult. Book 2 is a book of thinksheets. Similar to worksheets, these activity sheets help kids practice and think about the ideas they're learning. The thinksheets are meant to be used with adult guidance.

Social Thinking is a unique teaching methodology in which children are taught, in a concrete manner, to think in a social way. In other words, Social Thinking helps children think about the people around them and their choices and behavior in varying situations to determine what action or response is best. Social Thinking emphasizes that we can't learn one right answer for each situation, but rather we need to use our eyes, ears, brains, memory, and situational cues to figure out what to do in the moment. This is a very different concept from social skills teaching in that the emphasis isn't on mastery of discrete skills but on learning to think and problem solve at a social level. Social Thinking differs from social skills teachings by giving individuals specific thinking strategies they can use prior to social communication and interaction. The goal is to empower children to look at and think about social situations on their own and subsequently not need to rely on overly specific rules or rote behaviors.

As we work through this two-book set, I'll let you know which Social Thinking concepts and vocabulary we're learning. I'll also send home the completed thinksheets so you can stay connected to the content being used with your child.

You're also invited to purchase this two-book set and learn to use the Social Thinking Vocabulary terms outside the classroom with your child. You'll likely discover more teaching opportunities when you're with your child and become more familiar with the ideas as you explore them together.

More information on the Social Thinking Methodology, the Social Thinking® Vocabulary, and the various products they offer can be found at their website, www.socialthinking.com. You can also purchase a copy of this set there, read free articles, access their eLearning/online courses, find out about their face-to-face conferences, or sign up for their informative newsletter.

We're excited about this new learning opportunity and invite you to contact us with any questions or with examples from home that you feel demonstrate a particular Social Thinking concept.

Sincerely,

_____

Teacher/Therapist

Chapter 1
Extension Activities & Thinksheets

What Is Social Thinking?

Social Thinking or NOT?

In this chapter, students are becoming familiar with the idea of social thinking, what it means, and how it's different from other types of thinking and learning.

1. To begin, write several learning topics, some factual in nature and some social, on index cards (one topic per card). It's great to use factual topics that are meaningful to your students (such as dinosaurs, geography, or spelling words) and social topics you've noticed they struggle with (such as personal space, waiting for their turn, or the volume of their voice).

2. Give each student a blank piece of paper and ask them to fold it in half vertically. At the top on the left, have them write "Social Thinking topic." At the top on the right, have them write "NOT a Social Thinking topic."

3. Remind students that Social Thinking topics have to do with other people and ourselves when we're around other people, whereas NOT Social Thinking topics are facts that can be gathered using books or the Internet.

4. Have the students take turns picking a card from the deck and showing it to the group.

5. Invite discussion about which column the topic should go in.

6. When considering each topic, give students plenty of time to think, reassure them it's okay if they're unsure of the answer, and encourage them to ask the group for help if they want it.

7. Once a consensus is reached, have each student write that topic in the appropriate column on her piece of paper.

   Note: Be sure to make modifications for students who have fine motor difficulties so that the writing itself isn't an additional demand. For example, the group could work from one paper and students who enjoy writing or are strong writers could take turns being the scribe for the group.

8. If you want, make photocopies of the final product for students to take home.

28

Thinking About Social Thinking

Circle your answer in each of the thinking exercises below.

1. The type of thinking your brain does about other people is called
   world | social | self

2. We can use social thinking to figure out:
   a. What people mean when they point at something or use other nonverbal communication
   b. What someone is planning to do next
   c. What someone is feeling
   d. What I'm supposed to do or say
   e. All of the above

3. **Agree/Disagree:** People learn all they need to learn about social thinking by the time they're 15 years old.

4. **Agree/Disagree:** It's okay to make mistakes while we learn to become better social thinkers.

5. **Agree/Disagree:** A young child and an older child usually have the same social thoughts about a situation.

6. Another way to talk about people improving their social smarts is to say they're getting more **mature | talkative | self-centered.**

7. **Agree/Disagree:** I can use my social thinking to help me figure out which people I don't want to spend time around.

8. **Agree/Disagree:** I'll learn everything I need to learn about being a social thinker in a classroom with a teacher.

9. **Agree/Disagree:** When I use my social thinking skills to consider the thoughts and feelings of others, people will feel good around me and have good thoughts about me.

10. One really important reason to get better at social thinking is that I'll learn

    _____.

29

Using Social Thinking To Figure Out What People Are Communicating

For each picture, use your social thinking to figure out what each person is communicating with his or her body. Write down your answers on the blank lines provided.

The librarian: _____

The boys at the door: _____

The girl: _____

The mom: _____

The dad: _____

The mom: _____

The kids: _____

The teacher: _____

The boy with the blue shirt: _____

Using Our Social Smarts

When we use our social thinking, we are thinking about others in a situation, how they may be feeling, and what they might be thinking.

★ **Read each set of situations below and then decide which person or persons are using social thinking skills. Circle your answer.**

AT THE GROCERY STORE

Situation A. A girl is running down the aisle of a store with her mother chasing her.

Situation B. A girl is helping her mother push the shopping cart.

AT HOME IN THE KITCHEN

Situation A. A kid is standing in the middle of the kitchen floor yelling, "Get me a drink!" to his father who is cooking dinner.

Situation B. A kid is watching his dad cook dinner. He says, "Hey dad, I'm thirsty. Can I get a juice box from the fridge?"

IN LINE AT SCHOOL

Situation A. A group of students is calmly and quietly walking down the hallway in a line following the teacher.

Situation B. A group of students is walking down the hallway in a line following the teacher. Two of the students are running next to the line and tossing a ball back and forth.

IN LINE AT SCHOOL

Situation A. Two students bump into each other in the cafeteria. They look at each other and say, "Sorry."

Situation B. Two students bump into each other in the cafeteria. One student says, "Hey, watch where you're going weirdo!"

Using Our Social Smarts

IN THE CLASSROOM

Situation A. Two students are talking to each other while seated at their desks. Their teacher is at the front of the class explaining a math problem.

Situation B. Two students are seated next to each other at their desks while their teacher explains a math problem at the front of the class. One student whispers to the other, "I'll talk to you at lunch."

OUTSIDE NEAR WHERE YOU LIVE

Situation A. A girl's mom asks her to take some mail that was delivered to them by mistake to the neighbor across the street. The girl rings the doorbell, waits for the neighbor to answer the door, and gives her the mail with a smile.

Situation B. A girl's mom asks her to take some mail that was delivered to them by mistake to the neighbor across the street. The girl rings the doorbell but then sees a friend riding by on his bike. She drops the mail on the front step and runs to catch up with her friend.

33

Chapter 2
Extension Activities &
Thinksheets

Social Thinking

=

Flexible Thinking

Same Thing, Different Way

Present the students with a list of activities that span several different contexts or situations.

Ask them on their own, or as a group, to use their flexible thinking to brainstorm multiple ways to do the same thing. Some examples might be:

- Walking to the cafeteria. (Is there more than one route to get there?)

- Putting on shoes and socks. (We each know how we usually do it, but are there different ways or could you do this in a different order and still get the same result?)

- Hanging out with other students on the schoolyard. (This isn't just what you can do, but how you decide what to do. What are the different ways?)

- Making a peanut butter and jelly sandwich. (Could you execute the steps in a different order? Use different materials? How many different ways could you do this task?)

- Setting up a game board like Sorry or Monopoly. (Does it matter if you put game pieces on the board and then the cards? Does it matter when you give out the money as long as you do it before the game starts?)

- Saying "yes" in different ways. ("Yeah," "yup," "uh huh," head nod, thumbs up, smile and nod, "okey dokey," "you bet," etc.)

Identifying Ways To Think and Be Flexible

Everyone has different thoughts and feelings and may look at a situation in different ways. When we use our social thinking brains to think in different ways, we're using "flexible thinking."

This chapter talked about four ways to be flexible and use flexible thinking. We use our flexible brain to help us:

1. Understand that **people may say things that mean something different** from what we thought they meant.

2. Figure out why **people might do something** that we don't immediately understand.

3. Think about **what other people might want or need;** this might mean not getting our own way.

4. Know that sometimes **things have to happen in a different order or different way** than we're used to.

The following are examples of situations where a flexible brain is needed. Circle the number from the list above that best matches the type of flexible thinking needed.

1. When I get to school, my teacher tells me I look a little blue. I'm so mad at her! My skin isn't blue.

   For this situation, I need to use the flexible thinking described in: 1   2   3   4

2. My grandmother is visiting and cooked dinner tonight. She cooked macaroni and cheese, but it's different than how my mom makes it. I don't want to eat it.

   For this situation, I need to use the flexible thinking described in: 1   2   3   4

3. I'm waiting in line with my mother at the grocery store. A woman behind us pushes her cart and bumps into both me and my mom. I can't believe she did that!

   For this situation, I need to use the flexible thinking described in: 1   2   3   4

4. My teacher has asked the class for two volunteers to take a large box to the office. I raise my hand but he doesn't pick me. I never get picked to do anything!

   For this situation, I need to use the flexible thinking described in: 1   2   3   4

5. It was snowing this morning so our school day started two hours late. Because of this, we'll have a shorter lunch period. I'm not happy about this.

   For this situation, I need to use the flexible thinking described in: 1   2   3   4

6. I'm working with a partner on a science project on frogs. I think we should make a lifelike frog out of clay. My partner thinks we should do an animated video instead. Neither of us wants to change our opinion.

   For this situation, I need to use the flexible thinking described in: 1   2   3   4

7. Right after I said something in class, some other kids laughed. I wasn't telling a joke so I don't know why they're laughing.

   For this situation, I need to use the flexible thinking described in: 1   2   3   4

8. I'm getting ready to go to school, and my dad keeps looking at his watch. He tells me to "Shake a leg!" Why does he want me to stop getting ready and shake my leg?

   For this situation, I need to use the flexible thinking described in: 1   2   3   4

9. My grandmother is visiting for the weekend. My mom tells me I'll have to let her sleep in my room, and I'll sleep on the couch. Why can't she sleep on the couch instead of me?

   For this situation, I need to use the flexible thinking described in: 1   2   3   4

10. I'm going to the movies with my family. I want to see one movie, but my sister wants to see a different one. My mom reminds me that the last time we went to the movies I got to choose. But I really don't want to see the movie my sister is picking!

   For this situation, I need to use the flexible thinking described in: 1   2   3   4

FLexibLe Thinking in My Own Words

Read each situation below and fill in the blank or circle the best answer.

1. When I'm using flexible thinking, people are more likely to have

   _____ thoughts about me.

2. When others are being flexible around me, I might feel (circle all that apply):

   · **Relaxed**   · **Stressed**   · **Annoyed**   · **Impatient**   · **Frustrated**

   · **Happy**   · **Content**   · **Irritated**   · **Safe**   · **Comfortable**

3. When I'm using inflexible or stuck thinking, people are more likely to have

   _____ thoughts about me.

4. When others are using stuck thinking around me, I might feel (circle all that apply):

   · **Relaxed**   · **Stressed**   · **Annoyed**   · **Impatient**   · **Frustrated**

   · **Happy**   · **Content**   · **Irritated**   · **Safe**   · **Comfortable**

In your own words, describe what a flexible thinking and stuck thinking response would be to each of the following situations.

5. I'm doing my homework at the kitchen table. My mom wants me to move so she can set the table for dinner.

   A flexible thinking response would be to _____

   _____

   A stuck thinking response would be to _____

   _____

39

FLexibLe Thinking in My Own Words

6. We have a substitute teacher at school one day who tells us our reading time will be after our quiz. We usually have it before the quiz.

   A flexible thinking response would be to _____

   _____

   A stuck thinking response would be to _____

   _____

7. I'm going to play a board game with some other kids in my class. I really want to go first, but so does everyone else.

   A flexible thinking response would be to _____

   _____

   A stuck thinking response would be to _____

   _____

8. My dad asks me to rake the leaves on Saturday morning. I wanted to spend the morning skateboarding with my friends.

   A flexible thinking response would be to _____

   _____

   A stuck thinking response would be to _____

   _____

FLexibLe Thinking in My Own Words

9. I'm at my locker in between classes. It's really crowded and a student walking by knocks my books right out of my hands.

    A flexible thinking response would be to _____

    _____

    A stuck thinking response would be to _____

    _____

10. My sister has been grouchy all day. My mom says to her, "It looks like you got up on the wrong side of the bed this morning!"

    Flexible thinking would help me know that my mom really means _____

    _____

    Stuck thinking in this situation would make me think my mom means _____

    _____

41

Who Looks Like They're Being FLexibLe?

Look at the illustration below. It shows several groups of kids working together. Circle the people you notice who are using flexible thinking. Think about why you made the choices you did and be prepared to talk about them.

Chapter 3
Extension Activities & Thinksheets

Social Thinking®
Vocabulary

Social Thinking Vocabulary Deck

This activity promotes frequent and consistent review of the vocabulary presented in this chapter.

1. Write each term discussed in the chapter on an index card. You could make it more engaging by using colored index cards or colored text.

2. If you want, you can glue a picture or image on each card to match the idea and help kids tune into the words presented. For example, for Thinking and Feeling, you could add a picture of "The Thinker" statue and a heart. For Using Social Memory, you could place an image of a photo album. (Many free images are available online.)

3. Explain to students that this set of cards is the Social Thinking Vocabulary deck.

4. At the beginning of each session, ask one student to choose a card from the deck.

5. Ask the group to talk about or explain, in their own words, what that term means. Acknowledge their ideas, and supplement their answers with your own explanations to help fine-tune the ideas and present the important points for the students to retain.

This activity is a more demanding task in terms of expressive language, so be sure to make it a group collaboration. Share your own knowledge and thoughts generously to model possible answers. You can continue to do this activity as you move through different chapters. Keep the activity quick by limiting it to one card per session; this establishes a nice routine, delivers the information you want on a repeated basis, and optimizes the students' attention to the task.

Thinking and Feeling

> We are constantly thinking about things and the thoughts in our heads come in lots of sizes. We can have big thoughts, medium thoughts, and small thoughts. Feelings come in different sizes, too!

Read the question below and circle your answer.

1. We have thoughts about:
   a. People who are around us
   b. People who we remember
   c. Our friends
   d. Our family
   e. People who we don't know but have seen
   f. All of the above

In each situation below, decide if the person is probably having a BIG thought or a little thought and circle that answer. A BIG thought may be hard for the person to get out of his head. A little thought is a thought that will go away quickly on its own.

2. A girl sits at her desk in her classroom. She has a thought: "I'm SOOOO hungry! When will it be lunchtime?"

   Probably a BIG thought | Probably a little thought

3. Some kids are in the cafeteria and a fire alarm is going off. They have thoughts such as: "What IS that?," "Is that a fire alarm?," and "What are we supposed to do now?"

   Probably a BIG thought | Probably a little thought

4. Two kids are on a playground playing catch. A dog is barking off in the distance. The kid who is about to throw the ball has the thought: "Sounds like a dog. I can tell he is far away...."

   Probably a BIG thought | Probably a little thought

Thinking and Feeling

5. A student is at her desk writing with a pencil. She has the thought: "Oh no! My pencil point broke... but I can go sharpen it."

   Probably a BIG thought | **Probably a little thought**

⭐ **Think about the situations described in 2–5 above. Circle the feeling that probably goes with it.**

If your thought is "I'm SOOO hungry," you probably feel

    really hungry | **sleepy.**

If your thought is "Is that a fire alarm?," you might feel

    sad | **nervous.**

If your thought is "Sounds like a dog. I can tell he's far away," you might feel

    frustrated | **okay.**

If your thought is "My pencil point broke... but I can go sharpen it," you might feel

    really angry | **neutral.**

Agree/Disagree: Our thoughts usually make us feel different ways.

Using Your Senses To Figure Things Out

> Our senses send invisible signals to our brain about what's going on around us. This helps us become better social thinkers and social problem solvers.

1. Circle the senses that are important for social thinking:
   a. Seeing/Eyes
   b. Hearing/Ears
   c. Tasting/Tongue
   d. Touching/Skin
   e. Smelling/Nose

⭐ **Here are some examples of how you use your senses to figure out things about other people. For each example, circle one or more senses that are being used.**

2. I hear my teacher laughing and figure out that she probably thinks something is funny. I'm using my sense of:

   Seeing/Eyes | Hearing/Ears | Tasting/Tongue | Touching/Skin | Smelling/Nose

3. My teacher comments on the time by saying, "Oh look! It's 11:30 already!" He says this while he's looking at the class schedule. I figure out he needs to get us ready for lunch. I'm using my sense of:

   Seeing/Eyes | Hearing/Ears | Tasting/Tongue | Touching/Skin | Smelling/Nose

4. My teammate gives me a high five. I can tell she's happy that we just won our game. I'm using my sense of:

   Seeing/Eyes | Hearing/Ears | Tasting/Tongue | Touching/Skin | Smelling/Nose

5. My little brother pushed me after I changed the TV channel when he was watching a show he likes. I can tell he's upset with me. I'm using my sense of:

   Seeing/Eyes | Hearing/Ears | Tasting/Tongue | Touching/Skin | Smelling/Nose

Using Your Senses To Figure Things Out

6. I can't see it, but I know the front door just opened and closed. All of a sudden I get a whiff of pizza in the air. My dad yells, "Dinner!" I figure out that he just got home and brought us pizza. I'm using my sense of:

Seeing/Eyes | Hearing/Ears | Tasting/Tongue | Touching/Skin | Smelling/Nose

7. Use your senses to notice where you are right now. For example, look at the people or person you're with, look at the things in the room, or look out the window. Notice if there are any smells in the air. Take a moment to hear any noises both near and far away. Now, share one thing you've just figured out using your senses in this moment.

_____

_____

_____

_____

_____

_____

Thinking With Your Eyes

Thinking with your eyes means you look at things that are going on around you and use your brain to figure out what the clues mean. When you're not sure about something or not sure what to do, you can often figure this out by thinking with your eyes. We'll have more practice on thinking with your eyes in Chapter 5, but let's start here with one exercise on this vocabulary term.

1. Thinking with your eyes is another way of talking about:
   a. Using your eyes and brain together to figure out what's going on around you
   b. Listening to your teacher
   c. What you're thinking
   d. Taking a test

2. I can think with my eyes to figure out:
   a. What to do in a certain situation
   b. How people might feel
   c. Both a and b

3. **Agree/Disagree:** I can think with my eyes to figure out what other people might do next.

4. Explain why you chose that answer in #3.

   _____

   _____

5. **Agree/Disagree:** Only the person talking in a group needs to think with his/her eyes.

49

Hidden Rules and The Situation

In each situation there are hidden rules. We call them "hidden" because people don't talk about every little thing you need to say or do when you're in the situation. It's expected that you figure out the hidden rules so you know what to do. This helps others feel calm when around you.

⭐ **Read the situations below and think about how to answer each question using your social smarts!**

1. When thinking about a situation, it's important to keep in mind (circle all that apply):
   a. Where you are
   b. Who you're with and your relationship to them
   c. What you had for breakfast that morning
   d. What's happening at the moment
   e. Your favorite color

2. Hidden rules are a set of rules that most people agree upon related to a particular

   _____ .

   Hidden rules tell people how to _____ in that situation.

3. **Agree/Disagree:** All situations have the same hidden rules.

4. If I don't know the hidden rules for a situation I'm in, I can (circle all that apply):
   a. Think with my eyes: Look around and see what other people are doing.
   b. Listen with my ears: Figure out what other people are saying or talking about.
   c. Assume there aren't any hidden rules. I can do whatever I want.
   d. Ask a friend or adult for help figuring this out.

50

5. Below are some situations and hidden rules. Read the situations, then read all the hidden rules. Draw a line from the hidden rule to the situation it probably goes with.

THE SITUATION	HIDDEN RULES
I just lost a tennis match.	Try not to bump into others. Keep my body an arm's length away from the person in front of me. Don't yell out things like, "This line is moving too slow!"
My teacher says it's time for quiet reading.	Take out a book and read quietly at my desk.
I'm standing in line at a fast food restaurant waiting to order my food.	Use a fork; don't eat with my fingers. And use a napkin because it's probably messy.
My family and I are eating spaghetti and meatballs at our neighborhood Italian restaurant.	Say hello with a wave instead of saying, "Hi!"
I see a friend across the room as I enter the library. I want to greet her.	Keep my cool, don't get mad, and go congratulate the person who won.

6. **Agree/Disagree:** I only have to think about hidden rules when I'm at school.

7. When I follow the hidden rules of a situation, it helps others feel (circle one).

   comfortable | **uncomfortable**

Using Social Memory

> We keep information we know about other people in our brain. That way when we see these people again, we can call up what we know to find things to talk about with them. This helps others have good thoughts about us, and it shows others we're thinking about them!

1. Fill in the blank: Using our social memory means that we're using our brain to

   _____ things about people and situations.

2. **Agree/Disagree:** It's a good idea to use your social memory of others when you're with them.

3. **Agree/Disagree:** Social memory helps us remember what other people like and don't like.

⭐ **Read the following social thoughts in the left column. Draw a line from that thought to the social memory it goes with best.**

SOCIAL THOUGHTS	SOCIAL MEMORIES
You think your teacher is nice.	At dinner last night, she pushed her plate away and made a "yuk!" face after your mother put some broccoli on it.
You think your sister doesn't like broccoli.	This morning she was lying down on the couch and your dad helped you get ready for school. Usually your mom helps.
You think your classmate really likes Star Wars.	She smiled and said "Great work!" when she handed back your homework yesterday.
You think people get annoyed when someone talks during a movie.	Yesterday she smiled while telling the class, "Great job lining up quietly!"
You think your mother isn't feeling well.	Last time you went to the movies, you talked to your friend in a regular voice during the movie. Several people told you to be quiet!
You think your teacher likes it when the class lines up quietly.	He's always talking about Yoda and the other day he wore a Star Wars shirt.

Making Smart Guesses

> Sometimes when you're in a situation you have to make a guess about what to say or what to do. When you don't have a lot of information about the situation, you might make a silly guess (also called a wacky guess). But when you have some information, or you can think with your eyes to find some clues, you can make a smart guess.

For questions 1–4, decide whether you would have to make a silly guess or if you have enough information to make a smart guess. Circle your answer. When you're done, discuss your answers with each other, as some answers might be different!

1. On your walk home from school you see a moving van parked in front of the house next door to yours. You wonder where your neighbors are going.
   a. I would have to make a silly guess.
   b. I have enough information to make a smart guess.

2. A classmate of yours is having a birthday party. As she hands you an invitation she says, "Guess where my party is!"
   a. I would have to make a silly guess.
   b. I have enough information to make a smart guess.

3. Your teacher is out sick and you have a new substitute. You wonder if he'll let the class watch a movie.
   a. I would have to make a silly guess.
   b. I have enough information to make a smart guess.

4. You weren't in school today (Thursday) and you're wondering if you'll have your weekly math quiz tomorrow. The class has had a math quiz every Friday since the beginning of the school year.
   a. I would have to make a silly guess.
   b. I have enough information to make a smart guess.

Making Smart Guesses

5. If your teacher tells you to do something, and you're not sure what she means, what are some things you could do to help you make a smart guess? (Circle all that apply.)

   a. Look at what other people are doing

   b. Listen to what other people are saying

   c. Think back to a similar event in your past

   d. Find out what's for lunch in the cafeteria that day

   e. Ask your teacher for help

   f. Ask to go to the bathroom

Make some smart guesses about what's going on in these next three situations:

6. I notice my friend came into the classroom today with a big smile on her face. She has a medal around her neck. I remember that last week she said she was going to be in a gymnastics competition. What's my friend so happy about?

   _____

7. I notice my teacher keeps glancing out the window. During morning announcements, I remember the principal saying something about a fire drill. What's my teacher probably thinking about in this situation?

   _____

8. I remember that a classmate has been out of school for several days. She's back at school today but keeps putting her head down on her desk. My teacher comes over to her every so often to ask how she's feeling. What can I figure out about my classmate? How is my teacher probably feeling about her?

   _____

   _____

54

Chapter 4
Extension Activities & Thinksheets

We All Have Feelings

Noticing Body Language and Emotions in Animated Clips

1. Watch an age-appropriate short video clip and identify emotions of the characters at different points in the story.

   - Two favorites are *Shaun the Sheep* and *Pingu*. Video clips of both can be found online on sites such as YouTube. In these animated shorts, which are about five to ten minutes long, the characters communicate primarily through body language and tone of voice. Students always have fun watching these.

   - *Phineas and Ferb* is another show that's popular and humorous for most age groups. Although the characters speak within episodes, there are many opportunities to notice the exaggerated body language and emotions of characters such as Candace and evil Dr. Doofenshmirtz and to notice how their emotions may change quickly when their plans are thwarted. (Note: When choosing a *Phineas and Ferb* clip, be sure to preview it ahead of time. Most of the shows contain good, clean fun but there are a few isolated scenes in which Dr. Doofenshmirtz is in his underwear. Although intended to be humorous, it may not be a good choice for the group.)

2. Pause the clip along the way to spotlight what emotion a character may be feeling based on his or her body language and the context.

3. You can also use this activity to practice the idea of making smart guesses. Because the characters use mostly prosody and body language to communicate, viewers must constantly make smart guesses about what they think the characters are saying to each other. Pause the clips to give students a chance to make these smart guesses as a group.

For more ideas on teaching social concepts with clips from the media or YouTube, see the book *Movie Time Social Learning* by Anna Vagin (Think Social Publishing, 2013).

56

Identifying Our Own Feelings in Different Situations

> How people feel inside affects how they react to things and people around them. Before we can figure out how other people feel in different situations, we have to understand our own feelings.

For each situation that follows, **draw a picture of your face to show how you might feel in the social situation. Then choose an emotion from the Word Bank that best matches your feelings and write that word next to the picture.** Remember, there's no right or wrong way to do this! We all have different feelings so it's okay if you choose different words than your classmates do!

My teacher gives me my math quiz back and says, "Good job! You got most of the questions right."

I probably feel _____

WORD BANK:

happy, sad, excited, mad, surprised, uncomfortable, frustrated, disappointed, scared, okay

Identifying Our Own Feelings in Different Situations

Other kids invite me to play a game that I really want to play.

I probably feel _____

My schedule changes unexpectedly! We were supposed to do a science experiment, but we're having reading instead.

I probably feel _____

WORD BANK:

happy, sad, excited, mad, surprised, uncomfortable, frustrated, disappointed, scared, okay

IdenTifying Our Own FeeLings
in DiffereNT SiTuaTions

It's raining so we can't go outside at lunch.

I probably feel _____

I answer my teacher's question and she says,
"That's right! Good thinking."

I probably feel _____

WORD BANK:
happy, sad, excited, mad, surprised, uncomfortable, frustrated, disappointed, scared, okay

---

59

Identifying The Feelings of Others in Different Situations

Now that we've done some thinking about our own feelings in different situations, we can think about how others might feel in different situations. In this thinksheet let's do that. Let's practice thinking about the emotions that OTHERS have when they're around you in different situations.

 For each situation that follows:

1. Read the situation and imagine yourself in it. Then draw a simple face that shows how the **other person** mentioned might feel in that situation.

2. Choose an emotion from the Word Bank that best matches how that person(s) might feel in that situation. Write that word in the space provided.

I'm in class and I know the answer to my teacher's question. I raise my hand and wave it around and before the teacher calls on anyone, I blurt out the answer.

My teacher probably feels _____

WORD BANK:

happy, sad, excited, mad, surprised, uncomfortable, frustrated, disappointed, scared, okay

Identifying The Feelings of Others in Different Situations

I'm in the cafeteria line waiting to pay for my lunch. I try not to bump into the kids in front or in back of me.

The other kids probably feel _____

While studying in the library, I get hungry so I take an apple from my backpack and start eating it.

The librarian probably feels _____

WORD BANK:

happy, sad, excited, mad, surprised, uncomfortable, frustrated, disappointed, scared, okay

Identifying The Feelings of Others in Different Situations

I'm working in a small group on a class project. I listen to my friends' ideas and together we decide what to do.

My friends probably feel _____

I'm playing softball with other students. When I strike out, I start to yell that I never want to play again.

The other kids playing the game probably feel _____

WORD BANK:

happy, sad, excited, mad, surprised, uncomfortable, frustrated, disappointed, scared, okay

Identifying Feelings by Noticing Body Language and The Social Situation

> To figure out how other people feel, we can use our social detective skills. We do this by looking at other people's faces and their facial expression or by looking at their bodies to see if they look relaxed or if their muscles look tight. We can also look at their gestures to see what they're doing with their different body parts to give us more information. This is called reading "body language."

★ Here are some problems to solve! See if you can figure out what each person is feeling based on body language and these social situations. Write down the main emotion from the Word Bank you think the person is feeling.

Hint: The situation is described first, in blue. This helps give you the context. The rest of the text describes the person's body language.

AT SCHOOL

1. My teacher is talking to the class but several students are talking to each other instead. His voice is getting louder, his eyebrows are scrunched, and his hands are clenched together tightly. He's probably feeling

   _____ .

2. I'm on the schoolyard. Some kids are playing a game that has two teams. One team screams loudly, saying things like "Woo hoo!" and "Yeah!" That team jumps up and down and tosses a ball in the air. They're probably feeling

   _____ .

WORD BANK:
angry, frustrated, happy, embarrassed, sad, terrified, proud, disappointed, excited, relaxed, tired

3. It's lunchtime and one of the big bullies on campus just knocked over a student's tray of food. **The student is probably feeling**

_____.

4. The boy who has the locker next to mine can't get his locker open. It's almost time for class. He hits the locker, then kicks it. He's probably feeling

_____.

AT HOME OR IN THE COMMUNITY

1. I'm at my best friend's birthday party. She opens up a gift from her grandmother and it's the exact new tablet she wanted. She's probably feeling

_____.

2. I'm watching television. My mother is yelling something to me from the other room. I'm not listening to what she's saying. I notice that her voice is getting louder and louder, and her tone of voice doesn't sound friendly. My mom probably feels

_____.

3. My older brother just got home from sports practice. He's limping, goes to his room, and slams the door. He's probably feeling

_____.

4. My father is cooking dinner and I offer to set the table. He smiles and uses a very friendly tone of voice to say, "That would be great!" He's probably feeling

_____.

WORD BANK:
angry, frustrated, happy, embarrassed, sad, terrified, proud, disappointed, excited, relaxed, tired

64

Talking About Feelings in My Own Words

What two things can I notice to help me figure out how someone is feeling?

1. _____

2. _____

Why is it important to let others know how I'm feeling? _____

_____

Describe some body language I might notice in myself or others that's associated with each feeling:

Happy _____

Nervous _____

Mad _____

Disappointed _____

Tired _____

Circle the best answer:

When we make others feel good, they'll probably remember us as being

friendly | **mean** | **hungry.**

If we do something that makes others upset, they may remember us as being

nice | **rude** | **tired.**

WhaT Are They FeeLing?

Instructions: Look at the picture above. There are lots of clues about the situation, what's going on, and how people are feeling.

Pick out five people in the picture who have a number on or next to them and write down what you think each person is feeling and how you know that. For extra practice, do this for all seven people!

What Are They Feeling?

I think person _____ is feeling _____

because _____

I think person _____ is feeling _____

because _____

I think person _____ is feeling _____

because _____

I think person _____ is feeling _____

because _____

I think person _____ is feeling _____

because _____

I think person _____ is feeling _____

because _____

I think person _____ is feeling _____

because _____

67

Thinking About The Size of Our Feelings

> We can have many different types of feelings AND our feelings can also come in different sizes. Sometimes we might feel a little sad and other times we might feel really, really sad, depending on the situation, what's going on, and just how we feel that day. Sometimes we don't have much of a feeling at all, which we call "neutral" or being "okay."

 Read the following situations and circle the answer that you think best fits the situation.

1. **Agree/Disagree:** My feelings can change over the course of the day.

2. **Agree/Disagree:** Different people may have different size feelings in response to the same situation.

3. **Agree/Disagree:** It's okay to feel what I feel.

4. My neighbor won a lot of money in the lottery. He probably feels
   really happy | a little happy.

5. My friend's dog ran away. He loves his dog a lot. He might feel
   very sad | just a little sad.

6. My classmate's friend borrowed my homework and didn't give it back. I might feel
   really annoyed | a little annoyed.

7. The best player on our soccer team just broke his leg and can't play in the team finals. He might feel
   a little frustrated | very frustrated.

8. My dad just got a big promotion. He might feel
   really proud | a little proud.

In each of the pictures below and on the next page, your goal is to make a smart guess. Do you think the person is having a big feeling, a little feeling, or is feeling neutral? Use your social thinking! It's okay to have different opinions. Be ready to discuss your thoughts!

 **Circle one answer for each:**

The girl in front of the birthday cake is having a
big feeling | **little feeling** | **neutral feeling.**

The girl holding the green gift is having a
big feeling | **little feeling** | **neutral feeling.**

Remember: "Neutral" means you don't have very much of a feeling. It's similar to just feeling "okay."

Circle one answer:

The boy in the yellow shirt is having a
big feeling | **little feeling** | **neutral feeling.**

Thinking About The Size of Our Feelings

⭐ **Circle one answer for each:**

The mom is having a
big feeling | **little feeling** | **neutral feeling.**

The boy is having a
big feeling | **little feeling** | **neutral feeling.**

⭐ **Circle one answer for each:**

The grandmother is having a
big feeling | **little feeling** | **neutral feeling.**

The little girl with the pink dress is having a
big feeling | **little feeling** | **neutral feeling.**

The mom is having a
big feeling | **little feeling** | **neutral feeling.**

Chapter 5
Extension Activities & Thinksheets

Thinking With Your Eyes

Hiders and Finders

In this chapter, students learn about the Social Thinking Vocabulary concept "thinking with your eyes." This is a pivotal social concept that helps students learn to use both their eyes and brain to figure out things. One way to make learning this concept fun is to do select games and activities without talking at all, to emphasize how much information related to context and communication is nonverbal.

This activity is called **Hiders and Finders.**

1. Set two opaque paper cups upside down on a table, a few inches apart.

2. Find a small item of interest that could fit under a cup. Examples might be a coin, goldfish crackers, or a pair of dice.

3. Secure the group's attention and let them know you're going to hide the item under one of the cups, but first you'll choose the "finder" using only body language. Explain that if the student thinks you're choosing him or her, the person should say "Is it me?" (In future rounds you might select a different response the student can show that doesn't involve language.)

4. Cue your students to think with their eyes, reminding them that our eyes are like arrows. What our eyes point to indicates what a person may be thinking about or is interested in.

5. When the students are all looking at you, use body language to choose one person. For the first round of the game, you may want to use body language that's typically easy to read such as a distal point. However, as you get into the game and the students know what to expect, you can explore using more subtle body language such as a directed head nod (pointing your chin toward the person you have in mind), or even simply eye gaze directed at that person.

6. When the student in question asks, "Is it me?" you may use a head nod or thumbs up to indicate yes.

7. Ask the "finder" to close his or her eyes. Hide your item under one of the cups.

8. Take a moment to use declarative language to comment upon the contrasting information in everyone's brains at that moment as it's a great opportunity to illustrate theory of mind: "Right now, the finder doesn't know what cup I'm choosing because that person's eyes are closed and he can't see where I'm placing the item. But the rest of us do know where it is. We know, but the finder doesn't. We have different information in our brains right now!"

9. When ready, ask the finder to open her eyes and let the finder know that you will use only your eyes to help her figure out where the item is.

10. Once the student is looking at you, look at the cup where you've hidden the item and ask the finder to guess based on where you're looking.

11. Make sure to remind the student to keep her hands quiet and wait for your response before grabbing the cup. Even if the student doesn't guess correctly at first, this can be a great opportunity for problem solving and persistence in the moment. For example, if the student guessed incorrectly, prompt the person to look back at your gaze to reappraise your line of sight. This is great practice!

12. Continue the activity so each student has a chance to be the finder.

As easy as this activity may sound, some of your students may struggle with it while others may catch on pretty quickly. Here are some ways to modify for different levels of the social mind.

- Add more cups or arrange them differently based on each student's level of competence.

  - If it was easy for one student to determine your line of sight using only two cups, you could add one or two more cups.

  - If it's clear that using two cups was challenging for a student, try spreading them further apart on the table.

· Add body language as needed.

   · Scaffold the process a bit more for a student who finds the activity challenging by adding other body language such as a more obvious head position. If that's not enough try using your finger (or an object, such as a yardstick or a stick) to trace a point from your eyes to the cup. This reinforces the idea that your eyes are like arrows, pointing at what you're thinking about.

· Give students the opportunity to be the "hider" and to use their eyes and body language to select a "finder" and then hide the object under a cup and help the other student find it.

· Students generally enjoy playing this game with each other so once the game is familiar, have kids pair off and take turns with each other being the hider and finder. This can be a great opportunity for independent peer interaction and positive connection as well!

Thinking With Your Eyes – Part 1

> The Social Thinking term **think with your eyes** means we each use our eyes combined with our brain power to look at a situation and the people in the situation to figure out the meaning of what we're seeing. It's expected that when you're around others you think with your eyes. This is a social expectation that applies to just about everyone and helps us all try to make sense of what's going on around us!

Let's get you started thinking more about this topic with some basic ideas. Circle the answer you think is best.

1. **Agree/Disagree:** Reading a book or playing a game on my tablet or phone requires a lot of focus. At times like these, I don't have to think with my eyes about what's going on around me.

2. **Agree/Disagree:** To think with my eyes, I have to look around at the situation I'm in and try to notice where I am, what people are doing in the situation, what is expected of me, and how people are feeling.

3. **Agree/Disagree:** "Thinking with your eyes" and "making eye contact" are the same thing.

4. **Agree/Disagree:** Thinking with my eyes comes naturally; I never need to practice.

5. **Agree/Disagree:** People's eyes are like arrows. When I look at a person's eyes I can see what direction they're looking.

6. **Agree/Disagree:** It's possible to make a smart guess about what someone is thinking about, by noticing what they're looking at.

7. **Agree/Disagree:** If a person is looking at my teacher, it's less likely that person is thinking about me.

8. **Agree/Disagree:** When I think with my eyes, I can imagine that I'm a social detective, and I can start noticing social clues around me.

9. **Agree/Disagree:** "Observing" means writing down what people are doing in a situation.

10. **Agree/Disagree:** Thinking with my eyes when I'm talking to another person is expected behavior.

75

Thinking With Your Eyes — Part 2

> Let's continue learning about thinking with your eyes. Here are some questions to help you think a bit deeper about this topic.

⭐ **Thinking with my eyes is important because: (put an "X" next to all the reasons):**

_____ Thinking with my eyes can help keep me safe.

_____ Thinking with my eyes can help me figure out the group plan.

_____ Thinking with my eyes can help me become physically stronger.

_____ Thinking with my eyes can help me know what to do when I'm in a new situation.

_____ Thinking with my eyes can help me know how other people are feeling.

_____ Thinking with my eyes can help me find my way in the dark.

⭐ **Put an "X" next to all the statements you think are true:**

_____ People are expected to think with their eyes only at school.

_____ Kids can think with their eyes to figure out how their mom or dad is feeling.

_____ Thinking with my eyes is something I do just once, when I first enter a situation.

_____ To think with my eyes, I should borrow someone's glasses.

_____ When I think with my eyes, people will think I'm paying attention.

_____ Most people feel more comfortable when people around them are thinking with their eyes to help them figure out what to do as part of the group.

⭐ **When I think with my eyes I notice clues related to (put an "X" next to all that apply):**

_____ How people around me feel

_____ The place I'm in

_____ My favorite app

_____ What might be happening next

_____ What someone around me is doing

_____ What someone else is looking at

_____ A scavenger hunt coming up this weekend

⭐ **When I think with my eyes, I can figure out certain things. Imagine these situations and write down an example of a clue that might help you figure out each of these things.**

1. You see your sister or a friend sitting at the library reading a book. She looks very focused. What is one clue that would help you figure out what she's thinking?

   _____

2. You're shopping at a grocery store with your mom. You also see your teacher in the store. How will you know if your mom notices your teacher is in the store? What is one clue that would help you make this smart guess?

   _____

3. You notice your classmate playing a game on his device. What is one clue that would help you figure out what you could say to him?

   _____

Putting It All Together: Making Sure Your Eyes and Brain Work as a Team

Remember, we use our eyes to see, but then we must use our brains to think! For each of the clues that you "see" in the situations below, put your brain to work by "thinking" about what each might mean. This is thinking with your eyes in action! You help your eyes and brain *work together* to make a smart guess.

1. It's morning and stores are just starting to open on the shopping street. I see a lot of people gathered outside of one store. I can think with my eyes and make a smart guess that

   _____.

2. I know today we're going on a field trip and then I see my classmates getting their coats. I can think with my eyes and make a smart guess that

   _____.

3. I offer my friend some of my snack. I notice she shakes her head back and forth and lifts the palm of her hand toward my snack. I can think with my eyes and make a smart guess that

   _____.

4. The teacher says, "Let's move onto our math lesson" and I see other students putting away their social studies books and taking out their math books. Then I see many of them taking out a pencil. I can think with my eyes and make a smart guess that

   _____.

5. If I notice a friend looks tired and he is coughing or sneezing, I can think with my eyes and make a smart guess that

   _____.

6. It's November and I go grocery shopping with one of my parents. I see a lot of people buying turkeys at the grocery store. I can think with my eyes and make a smart guess that

_____.

7. I'm in class and I notice that kids are starting to pack up their books. I look at the clock and the time is 5 minutes before the school bell rings to tell us the school day is over. I can think with my eyes and make a smart guess that

_____.

8. I see one of my classmates start to limp in gym class, right after she jumped trying to shoot a basket. I can think with my eyes and make a smart guess that

_____.

9. If I'm at the mall and I notice that the place where my favorite store has always been is now empty, I can think with my eyes and make a smart guess that

_____.

10. If I come into my class and see that everyone is huddled around the class aquarium where we've been monitoring the progress of a pregnant fish, I can think with my eyes and make a smart guess that

_____.

Name: _____   Date: _____

Being a Social Detective

Being a social detective means we use our eyes, ears, and other senses to notice other people and what's happening around them. This helps you figure out what people are thinking and feeling and what you might do or say in a situation. Thinking with your eyes helps you become a better social problem solver.

Look at the picture below. There are lots of clues about what's going on. Use these clues to answer the questions on the next page. There might be more than one right answer for a question, so don't worry if you and your classmates come up with different answers!

Being a Social Detective

1. How do you think the kids know each other?

_____

_____

2. Who might the adult standing in front of the bus be?

_____

_____

3. Where do you think they might have been? Where might they be going?

_____

_____

4. What season could it be?

_____

_____

5. What's the name of the town where they are?

_____

_____

81

Thinking With Your Eyes To Find The Important Clues in a Situation

> You've been practicing with the idea of using your eyes to discover clues (clues are the important details in a situation) and using your brain to figure out what they mean. Smart social detectives are people who observe the clues and ignore extra details that are not important.

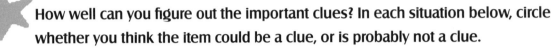 **How well can you figure out the important clues? In each situation below, circle whether you think the item could be a clue, or is probably not a clue.**

- ❏ **If you think it could be a clue, then practice being a social detective and make a smart guess about what it might mean.**

- ❏ **If it is not a clue, then just ignore the question about what the clue might mean!**

Situation 1: A student has come in late to lunch. Now the student has to be a social detective to figure out what's going on in the school cafeteria at lunchtime.

Kids are packing up their lunches. This **could be a clue/is probably not a clue.**
If it is a clue, what does this mean for how much time the student has to eat lunch?

_____

The lunchroom chairs are painted blue. This **could be a clue/is probably not a clue.**
If it is a clue, what does it mean related to what the student will eat for lunch?

_____

On the lunch menu blackboard there's a line through "Meatloaf" and there's no line through "Chicken Fingers." This **could be a clue/is probably not a clue.**
If it is a clue, what does this mean related to what the student will eat for lunch?

_____

Situation 2: A student is at the movie theater with a friend and his father.

The movie hasn't even started yet and the theater is packed! There are hardly any empty seats, but there are three seats together in the very last row. This **could be a clue/is probably not a clue.**
If it is a clue, what does this have to do with where the group will sit?

_____

The movie still hasn't started, but the lights just dimmed and previews start to play.
This **could be a clue/is probably not a clue.**
If it is a clue, what does this mean for how much time the group has to sit down?

_____

Two people are talking loudly after the movie starts. Several other people are looking at them with mad facial expressions. This **could be a clue/is probably not a clue.**
If it is a clue, what does this mean about how these people are feeling about the loud talkers?

_____

Thinking With Your Eyes To Know What To Say and When To Say It! Part 1

Before asking a question, making a comment, or starting a conversation with another person or a group, it's important to think with your eyes. Thinking with your eyes can help you know whether it's a good time to talk to someone, and if it is, it can help you figure out what to say. Let's practice these ideas!

Imagine yourself in each of the situations below. Think with your eyes to decide whether it's a good time to start a conversation with that person, or not. Circle your answer.

1. My friend is sitting alone at a table in the cafeteria. There's an empty seat next to her.

   I can think with my eyes to know that this **may be a good time to start a conversation/may not be a good time to start a conversation.**

2. My dad is on the phone.

   I can think with my eyes to know that this **may be a good time to ask my dad a question/may not be a good time to ask my dad a question.**

3. My teacher is talking quietly at her desk to another student. They both are looking pretty serious.

   I can think with my eyes to know that this **may be a good time to ask my teacher a question/may not be a good time to ask my teacher a question.**

4. I see my brother playing a basketball game. He has on a uniform and there are a lot of people watching the game.

   I can think with my eyes to know that this **may be a good time to tell my brother that I got an A on my test/may not be a good time to tell my brother I got an A on my test.**

5. Two kids are hanging out on the playground, laughing and talking. They look at me and wave. I can think with my eyes to know that this **may be a good time to join their conversation/may not be a good time to join their conversation.**

Thinking With Your Eyes To Know What To Say and When To Say It! Part 2

Let's think about what we can ask someone or say in a conversation by thinking with our eyes. For each of these situations, pay attention to the clues to figure out something you could say to the other person during your conversation.

1. I join my friend at lunch and see he is wearing a t-shirt that has a picture of Minecraft® on it. I like to play Minecraft. I could ask:

_____

2. I see my teacher at the grocery store. She has a little girl with her. She has told us she has a daughter. I could ask:

_____

3. I see that my classmates are all getting into groups to work on science projects. I see a group of three kids and they need one more kid to be part of their team. They're looking at me with friendly faces. I could walk over to them and ask:

_____

4. I notice that my mom is in the backyard planting some flowers. I could say:

_____

5. My sister comes home from a soccer tournament wearing an award medal around her neck. I could ask:

_____

85

More Practice Thinking With Your Eyes

Thinking with our eyes helps us figure out a situation. Practice thinking with your eyes in each of these situations. Write your answer in the space provided.

A mom is taking a boy to school and she's walking quickly. You're wondering what the big hurry is. Think with your eyes to see if you can figure out what's going on.

_____

_____

In the picture above, Josh, the boy on the right, can't remember what time Art starts. He can think with his eyes to figure this out by....

_____

_____

Think With Your Eyes About Different Situations

⭐ **Picture the situations that follow in your mind and imagine yourself in them. Then write your responses in the space provided.**

1. You just walked into gym class. You're a few minutes late, and you see other students lined up taking turns shooting a basketball. If you think with your eyes, what can you probably figure out to do?

   _____

   _____

2. You're sitting at a table with your family at a restaurant. You need to go to the bathroom but don't know where it is. How could you think with your eyes to figure this out?

   _____

   _____

3. You've just finished your work at your desk. You can't remember what your teacher said you should do when you're done. How could you think with your eyes to figure this out?

   _____

   _____

4. You see your mom talking on the telephone. You know she was waiting for someone to call with some news. You wonder if the news is good news or bad news. How could you think with your eyes to figure this out?

   _____

   _____

Chapter 6
Extension Activities & Thinksheets

Thinking About The Hidden Rules and Expected Behavior

Looking for The Hidden Rules

This activity can be done with photos, illustrations, or even with video.

1. Print large images (at least 5x7" or 8x10") of various social scenarios or have these ready to display on a tablet or a computer. (As mentioned above, many websites offer free images. For these, you may need to search for "waiting in line," "playground with students," and "classroom with students.")

2. Let the students know that as a group they should think with their eyes to figure out expected behavior in a few different settings you'll show them.

3. Show them the images one at a time and invite discussion about what the students notice *most* people are doing. Explain that because most people are doing the same or a similar thing, this is probably expected behavior for that place. For example, if you show them a photo of several people standing in line to get tickets at a movie theatre, talk about how people are standing, what they're doing with their bodies, whether or not they're talking, etc.

4. Ask the students to look again at the picture to see if they notice a sign that states these things. After noticing together that no such sign exists, emphasize that they're correct — these are "hidden rules" and it's expected behavior that we each figure them out on our own by thinking with our eyes.

5. After students have practiced this activity, invite them to create some new situations of their own to review. You could ask them to find different situations at school and take pictures of them with a camera, or their phone/tablet camera. Note that schools typically require parental permission before students are photographed so proceed with this activity only after necessary consents are in place.

6. After they've taken photos, ask the group to see if they can figure out the hidden rules of that situation.

Note: Students could instead take video of situations to discuss the hidden rules. First check your school's guidelines for video recording and any required permissions. Consider deleting the video once you and your students have finished discussing them.

90

Expected and Unexpected Behavior in a Situation

Expected behavior is behavior that most people do in a certain place or certain situation.

Unexpected behavior is the opposite. It's behavior that most people wouldn't do or shouldn't do in a certain situation.

⭐ Look at the picture below of people at the movies. There are 7 people who are using unexpected behavior. See how many you can find and then draw a circle around each person. Can you find them all?

91

Expected and Unexpected Behavior in a Situation

⭐ Now, let's talk more about this situation and expected/unexpected behaviors.

List 3 expected/okay behaviors when at the movies:

1. _____

2. _____

3. _____

List 3 unexpected/not okay behaviors when at the movies:

1. _____

2. _____

3. _____

List 3 (or more) feelings you or others might have when people at the movies show expected behavior:

1. _____

2. _____

3. _____

_____

List 3 (or more) feelings you or others might have when people at the movies show unexpected behavior:

1. _____

2. _____

3. _____

_____

Name: _____ Date: _____

Identifying Expected and Unexpected Behavior for Different Situations

Chapter 6: Thinksheet 2

Page 1 of 3

Let's have some fun practicing these ideas. Read the situations that follow and choose one situation each from school, home, and the community. Draw a picture, cut one out from a magazine, or find one on the Internet that shows possible expected and unexpected behaviors for each situation. Under each picture, draw an emotion face that shows how others may feel in response to that behavior.

SCHOOL

Choose and circle one of these situations. Or create your own situation below.

1. Checking out a book at the library

2. Working in a group on a project

3. Eating lunch in the cafeteria

4. Hanging up my coat and belongings in my locker

5. Think of my own situation and write it here: _____

_____

Picture of expected behavior	Picture of unexpected behavior
Emotion face:	Emotion face

Social Thinking and Me   93   ©2016 Think Social Publishing, Inc. • www.socialthinking.com

Identifying Expected and Unexpected Behavior for Different Situations

HOME

⭐ **Choose and circle one of these situations, or create your own below.**

1. Getting ready for bed

2. Eating dinner with my family

3. Watching TV with my mom or dad

4. Answering the telephone

5. Think of my own situation and write it here: _____

_____

Picture of expected behavior	Picture of unexpected behavior
Emotion face	Emotion face

COMMUNITY

Choose and circle one of these situations, or create your own below.

1. Waiting in the checkout line at the grocery store

2. Sitting in the waiting room at my doctor's office

3. Eating at a restaurant

4. Getting my hair cut

5. Think of my own situation and write it here: _____

_____

Picture of expected behavior	Picture of unexpected behavior
Emotion face	Emotion face

95

Name: _____ Date: _____

Exploring How Expected/Unexpected Behaviors Affect Feelings — Part 1

Our behaviors cause others to have thoughts and feelings about us. Let's think first about different situations at home or in the community.

⭐ Read and think about each situation below. In column 2 write three expected behaviors for each situation. For each behavior you wrote in column 2, draw a line to the feeling word that describes how others might feel in response to someone behaving that way.

Next, write down three unexpected behaviors for each situation in column 4. Draw a line to the feeling others may be having.

The Situation	Expected Behavior	How might others feel?	Unexpected Behavior
Watching a movie at home with my family.	1. 2. 3.	Happy Relaxed Neutral Upset Annoyed Uncomfortable	1. 2. 3.

96

The Situation	Expected Behavior	How might others feel?	Unexpected Behavior
Hanging out with my friends at one of their houses	1. 2. 3.	Happy Relaxed Neutral Upset Annoyed Uncomfortable	1. 2. 3.

The Situation	Expected Behavior	How might others feel?	Unexpected Behavior
Watching someone open presents at a birthday party	1. 2. 3.	Happy Relaxed Neutral Upset Annoyed Uncomfortable	1. 2. 3.

Name: _____   Date: _____

Exploring How Expected/Unexpected Behaviors Affect Feelings – Part 2

★ Now let's use our flexible thinking to think about different types of expected and unexpected behaviors at school. Follow the same directions as in the previous thinksheet.

The Situation	Expected Behavior	How might others feel?	Unexpected Behavior
Coming into my classroom to get ready to learn	1. 2. 3.	Happy Relaxed Neutral Upset Annoyed Uncomfortable	1. 2. 3.

The Situation	Expected Behavior	How might others feel?	Unexpected Behavior
My teacher explaining a new lesson	1. 2. 3.	Happy Relaxed Neutral Upset Annoyed Uncomfortable	1. 2. 3.

98

The Situation	Expected Behavior	How might others feel?	Unexpected Behavior
Having a substitute teacher for the day	1. 2. 3.	Happy Relaxed Neutral Upset Annoyed Uncomfortable	1. 2. 3.

The Situation	Expected Behavior	How might others feel?	Unexpected Behavior
Working in the class by myself	1. 2. 3.	Happy Relaxed Neutral Upset Annoyed Uncomfortable	1. 2. 3.

Exploring How Expected/Unexpected Behaviors Affect Feelings – Part 2

The Situation	Expected Behavior	How might others feel?	Unexpected Behavior
Lining up for the bus	1. 2. 3.	Happy Relaxed Neutral Upset Annoyed Uncomfortable	1. 2. 3.

The Situation	Expected Behavior	How might others feel?	Unexpected Behavior
Eating lunch in the cafeteria	1. 2. 3.	Happy Relaxed Neutral Upset Annoyed Uncomfortable	1. 2. 3.

Describing Expected and Unexpected Behaviors in Your Own Words

In this exercise you'll think more about expected and unexpected behaviors and feelings related to them. Think about a situation in your life. This may be something you do each day at school, at home, or even on the weekends. It could be a specific event, like going to soccer practice, or even something smaller, like eating breakfast or brushing your teeth. Have fun and be creative in the situation you choose!

★ To start, write down your situation in your own words. Next, think about different behaviors in that situation. Write down three expected and three unexpected behaviors in that situation.

The Situation: _____

Expected behaviors in this situation	Unexpected behaviors in this situation
1.	1.
2.	2.
3.	3.

★ Now, think about how behaviors are connected to feelings. Think about how the behaviors in this situation might make other people feel. List three feelings people might have in response to your expected behaviors, and then three feelings people might have in response to your unexpected behaviors.

Expected behaviors: feelings others might have	Unexpected behaviors: feelings others might have
1.	1.
2.	2.
3.	3.

101

Keep going! Let's make the connection between how people feel in response to your behaviors and how they treat you because of those feelings.

When you do expected behaviors, people may be nice to you. List three ways they might show how they feel. When you do unexpected behaviors, people may not be very nice to you. List three ways they might show that feeling.

In response to my expected behaviors: ways people may be nice to me	In response to my unexpected behaviors: ways people may not be very nice to me
1.	1.
2.	2.
3.	3.

Now, let's put it all together and connect behavior and feelings back to you! How people treat you often affects how you feel in the situation (happy, sad, frustrated, mad) or how you feel about yourself (proud, disappointed, angry). List three feelings YOU might have when people are nice to you (because you had expected behaviors). Then go back and list three feelings YOU might have when people are not nice to you (because you had unexpected behaviors).

My feelings when people are nice to me	My feelings when people are not nice to me
1.	1.
2.	2.
3.	3.

Connecting Thoughts, Feelings, and Behaviors in Expected/Unexpected Situations

As you get better at becoming a social detective, you may notice that there's a connection you can see between thoughts and behaviors, both in yourself and your own life, and in others. When you do what's expected, people tend to feel better about you and about being around you. Then they treat you nicer and this helps you feel good about yourself and others too. When you do what's unexpected, things don't go as well.

Let's see how these pieces fit together by filling out the chart on the next page. In Social Thinking we call this chart a "Social Behavior Map." This can help you see the connection between thoughts and feelings when behavior is expected and unexpected. Follow these steps:

1. Write in the situation. You can think of one on your own or ask for help from a peer or adult.

2. Choose one expected behavior for this situation and write that in the chart.

3. Choose one unexpected behavior for this situation and write that in the chart.

4. Choose one feeling people might have for each behavior and write those in the chart.

5. Choose one reaction people might have to their feeling and write that in. How are they nice? How are they not-so-nice in response to you?

6. Choose one of your own feelings when people are nice to you or not nice to you and add those to the chart.

7. Now review the two sections of the chart: the expected side and the unexpected side. Can you see the connection?

Connecting Thoughts, Feelings, and Behaviors in Expected/Unexpected Situations

The Situation: _____

Expected Behavior	How it might make other people feel	How people might treat me	How I feel about myself

Unexpected Behavior	How it might make other people feel	How people might treat me	How I feel about myself

(Adapted from *Social Behavior Mapping: Connecting Behavior, Emotions and Consequences Across the Day* by Michelle Garcia Winner, 2007. This helpful book has examples of filled-in Social Behavior Maps for many different situations to help students better understand how their behaviors affect the thoughts and feelings of others and how that, in turn, affects how our students feel about themselves. A really useful tool! Find the book and a poster template at www.socialthinking.com)

Chapter 7
Extension Activities & Thinksheets

Keeping My Body, Eyes, Ears, and Brain in The Group

Body In - Body OuT? Brain In - Brain OuT?

In Lesson 9 in *Think Social!,* Michelle presents an engaging activity using Play-Doh to demonstrate the idea of keeping one's body and brain in the group. It works well as a supplemental activity for this chapter. Another option is to use role play. Here's one example of a role play activity:

1. Let the students know that you're going to move to different places in the room, and you want them to decide as a team whether your body is in the group or not in the group.

2. Scoot your chair closer and further away from the table incrementally, or move sporadically to different places in the room. At each new position ask them, "How about now?"

3. Allow the students to come to a consensus and answer using the words "Your body IS in the group" or "Your body is NOT in the group." If moving back incrementally, note and label the place where your body moved from being in the group to being not in the group. For example, was it when you were about one arm's length away? This is important to highlight to the group.

You can do a similar role play to demonstrate "brain in the group."

1. Tell students they'll decide as a group whether your brain is in the group or not in the group.

2. Sit at the table and assume different positions that communicate you're thinking about the group or not thinking about the group. For example, put your head down, turn your body away, turn your body toward the group and smile, look at the speaker and nod, stare at the ceiling and hum, etc. For students who won't become too dysregulated by silliness, have a little fun by putting your head under the table, standing on a chair but looking at the group, or doing other silly things. At each new position, ask them if your brain is in the group or not.

3. For each different position, ask the students to discuss as a group what they want their answer to be.

As students become more adept at noticing when your body or brain is in the group/out of the group, have students take turns (or volunteer) to be the person demonstrating the concept. Students usually love doing this!

For review of both body in the group and brain in the group, you might also consider taking photos of the group during different activities and over time. Later, view these photos together to determine whose bodies/brains appear in the group versus whose bodies/brains appear not in the group. During any review of photos together, be sure to assume an objective, observational tone with your students, rather than a judgmental "right and wrong" way of describing their actions. Openly discuss what observable characteristics make a person appear in the group or not. Be sure to include teachers in these photos as well, so students don't feel they're the only ones in the spotlight!

Movie Theatre and Quiet Catch

One enjoyable way for elementary-aged students to practice the concept of keeping their body, eyes, ears, and brain in the group is to have them pretend they're at a movie theater. Although children engage in pretend play less as they grow older, they always seem to enjoy it when given the opportunity. Sharing imaginations is also a great way to allow students to exchange ideas and talk back and forth. Include props such as empty cups and toy or real food for the concession stand and tickets (either real raffle type tickets that can be easily found online or in a stationery store or ones made by the students).

1. Assign students roles such as concession stand worker, ticket taker, and moviegoer. Allow students to take turns in the different roles.

2. While moviegoers "purchase" tickets and refreshments from each other, they can practice turning their body toward the other people and showing they're thinking about what's being said by listening and responding to requests.

3. When students pretend to be in the theater, they can practice turning their body toward what the group is thinking about (the movie screen), thinking with their eyes to monitor others around them, keeping their body still, and staying quiet.

4. It can be especially motivating to students to pretend to watch the movie by showing them a short trailer on a tablet or a laptop. Just be sure to let them know they won't be watching the whole movie but only a short clip.

An activity for older students to reinforce listening behavior and paying attention is called **Quiet Catch.**

1. Have students get in pairs and stand or sit opposite each other.

2. Give each pair a tennis ball, pom pom, or another item to pass or toss.

3. Ask students to line up their bodies opposite each other about one arm's length away from each other. One holds the ball (or other object) and both students assume an attentive posture to each other.

4. When the ball holder notices with his eyes that the catcher is ready and is demonstrating listening behavior (looking at his partner, with shoulders, feet, etc. turned toward the partner, he is quiet and is thinking about the student who has the ball), the ball holder carefully tosses the ball.

5. Students should continue with this process until they master the toss or catch at this distance.

6. You can then add the challenge of asking the students to share information about a topic of choice. The tosser comments or asks a question, and doesn't toss the ball until she can really tell that the catcher has heard her (the catcher responds, makes a related comment, or nods his head in understanding).

7. The new tosser continues the conversation by adding another thought, being sure not to toss the ball until the new catcher is ready with his body and is thinking about what has just been said.

8. Keep in mind that the emphasis of this game is on slowing down our pace to notice our partner or adjust to our partner's pace. If students are tossing the ball quickly to each other, they'll miss the point. Provide praise and acknowledgement to those who take their time: "I love how you're going slow and taking your time to check in with each other!"

What Is a Group and Why Does Being Part of a Group Matter?

In this chapter we talked a lot about what it means to be part of a group and how we can show others we want to be included. Let's start with some review and then practice some of the concepts we learned.

Read and think about each exercise that follows. Fill in the blank or circle the answer you think is best.

1. A group is more than one person sharing the same _____ together.

2. **Agree/Disagree:** A group is at least 3 people.

Read the following and put a check mark next to all that apply.

3. A "group plan" is:

_____ A way we can talk about the reason everyone in that group is together

_____ A drawing, just like an architect's plan for a building

_____ What everyone tries to focus on when they're in a group together

_____ What everyone might be doing together, or a common activity that the people in the group are sharing

_____ Always said out loud and told to everyone in the group before they join

_____ Something we might have to figure out on our own when we join a group

WhaT Is a Group and Why Does Being Part of a Group MaTTer?

Chapter 7: Thinksheet 1

Page 2 of 2

It's important to think about the thoughts others have about us. Read the following thinking exercises and circle the answer you think is the best one.

4. It's important to keep my body and brain in the group because when I do this, other people will know that I am

   interested in them | **not interested in them.**

5. When my head or my body is turned away from the group, people probably will think I am

   interested in them | **not interested in them.**

6. When my body is part of the group, but I'm using my eyes to look all around, people may think I am

   thinking about what they're saying | **not thinking about what they're saying.**

7. When my body is in the group, and I say something that's related to what the group is talking about, others may think

   I'm listening and interested in what they're saying | **I don't care about what they're saying.**

110

Body in The Group:
What Does That Look Like?

When we're with others, it's expected behavior that we think about the people in the group and what the group is doing. One way we do this is by keeping our body, eyes, ears, and brain in the group. Let's practice thinking about this idea by noticing if these animals are in the group/out of the group.

⭐ **Look at each picture below. Decide if the animal circled has its body in the group or out of the group. Then see if you can make a smart guess about the group plan!**

☐ Body is in the group.

☐ Body is out of the group.

The group plan is probably to:

_____.

☐ Body is in the group.

☐ Body is out of the group.

The group plan is probably to:

_____.

111 ©2016 Think Social Publishing, Inc. • www.socialthinking.com

Using Our Body, Eyes, Ears, and Brain To Show Others We're in The Group

We use our bodies in many different ways to establish physical presence and let people know our plan is to be part of the group. This means we communicate with more than just our words! And, we also use our brain to help us listen and stay focused on what others are doing or saying.

When we don't keep our body, eyes, ears and brain in the group, others might have uncomfortable thoughts about us or wonder why we're even around them.

Look at the five boys below. They're all on the same swim team. Think about what the group plan might be and write that down. Next, decide if each boy's body, eyes, ears, and brain are in the group or out of the group and put a check mark in that box.

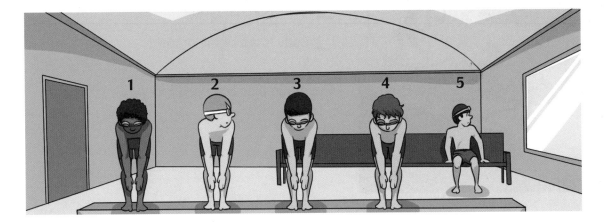

The group plan is probably to _____.

	Boy #1	Boy #2	Boy #3	Boy #4	Boy #5
Body is in the group					
Body is out of the group					
Eyes, ears, and brain are in the group					
Eyes, ears, and brain are out of the group					

More Practice on Body, Eyes, Ears, and Brain in The Group

⭐ **Read and think about the situations below. For each use simple sketches to show what keeping your body, eyes, ears, and brain in the group might look like. Then discuss whether the kids are showing expected or unexpected behavior in the situation.**

IN THE CLASSROOM

Draw 3 kids and a teacher. Show what it looks like if the kids have their bodies and brains in the group while listening to the teacher talk. Which behaviors are expected?

Draw the same kids and teacher but this time show what it looks like if one kid has his or her brain out of the group. Who is showing expected behavior and who is showing unexpected behavior?

113

AT THE MALL

Draw 4 boys or girls walking together side by side. Show what it looks like if the kids all have their bodies and brains in the group. Which behaviors are expected?

Draw the same 4 boys or girls walking together. This time show what it looks like if 2 kids have their brain out of the group and one kid has his or her body out of the group. Discuss which behaviors are expected and unexpected.

BONUS!

Pick your own situation and draw a picture showing a group and some of the kids with their body, eyes, ears, and brain in the group and some of the kids with their body, eyes, ears, or brain out of the group.

Next, select 2 kids and explain below which one is showing expected/unexpected behavior and why.

_____

_____

_____

_____

Adding Our Brains into The Group

When we notice social clues by thinking with our eyes and listening with our ears, we also need to figure out what it all means! This is where our brain helps us out. Our brain helps us make smart guesses to interpret what we think people are doing or feeling or what they might be planning to do next. This helps us figure out the group plan too!

Read the following situations and see if you can figure out the answers to fill in the blanks. If you need help, talk over the situations with an adult or a peer.

1. My teacher points toward the door and it's time for gym class. The group plan is

   probably to _____ .

   I can keep my body, eyes, ears, and brain in the group by doing this:_____

   _____ .

2. As I walk up to a group of friends in the cafeteria I see they're all starting to stand

   up and gather up their trays and backpacks. I can use my eyes, ears and brain to

   figure out their plan is to _____ .

   What would be one expected behavior I could use in this situation? _____

   _____ .

3. I'm telling a classmate about a great movie I saw over the weekend. I notice he

   keeps looking at his cell phone rather than looking at me. I can use my eyes and

   brain to figure out that he is probably _____ .

   Is the classmate's behavior expected or unexpected? _____ .

   What's one expected thing I could say or do in this situation? _____

   _____ .

Adding Our Brains into The Group

4. Our class is working in groups on our science projects. Jessica is sitting with

   our group but she's not doing any work. Instead she's making little noises

   and rubbing her head and then puts her head down on her desk.

   What can I figure out about the situation with Jessica by using my eyes, ears, and

   brain? _____ .

   What's one expected behavior I could show in this situation? _____

   _____ .

5. I'm having dinner at my friend's house with his mom, dad, and his sister. I have my

   body in the group and I'm using my eyes, ears, and brain to show others I'm

   interested. Everyone is talking about their upcoming trip to the Grand Canyon. I say,

   "Why would you go there when you could go to Death Valley instead?" Everyone

   stops talking and my friend kicks my leg under the table. What happened?

   If I use my eyes, ears, and brain even more I can figure out I_____

   _____ .

   What can I do that would be expected in this situation to make things better?

   _____ .

Using My Body and Brain To Listen While in a Group

When you're part of a group you're using different parts of your body AND your brain to listen to others and figure out the whole picture of a situation, or what someone is saying. It's a lot more than just using your ears to hear the words or sounds. It involves keeping your mouth, arms, hands, legs, and feet quiet and still. When we do this it actually helps our brain focus on what's being said! This sends a message to others that you're interested in what they're saying!

★ The students in these three pictures are working on a class science project. First, find students who are using their bodies to show others they're part of the group. Put a circle around those students.

Next, find students who appear to have their body, eyes, ears, or brain out of the group. Put a check mark next to those students. Be prepared to talk about your choices and why you made them.

118

Thinking About Expected Behaviors in Different Situations

When we listen with our brain and keep our body parts quiet and still, people can tell we're thinking about what they're saying. They'll have good thoughts about us when we do this!

Read the following situations. Decide if the person is using his or her body and brain to be part of the social situation and is showing expected behavior. Then make a smart guess about how the person in the situation might feel and what social thoughts that person might have. Circle or write in your answer.

1. My friend is telling me about her upcoming basketball game. I look at her, smile, and nod as she speaks.

   I am | **am not** showing expected behavior in this situation.

   My friend will think I **am** | **am not** interested in her basketball game.

   My friend will probably feel _____ and will have
   good | **uncomfortable** thoughts about me.

2. My teacher is writing a history assignment on the board. I'm playing with my hair and tapping my foot while I'm looking around the room.

   I am | **am not** showing expected behavior in this situation.

   My teacher will think I **am** | **am not** interested in the assignment.

   My teacher will probably feel _____ and will have
   good | **uncomfortable** thoughts about me.

120

3. I'm at my sister's dance recital with my family. I'm sitting in my seat, facing the stage, with my hands and feet still. I'm watching the dancers and thinking about the music.

I **am** | **am not** showing expected behavior in this situation.

My family will think I **am** | **am not** interested in the performance.

They'll probably feel _____ and will have **good** | **uncomfortable** thoughts about me.

4. I'm in the cafeteria sitting next to my friend. She's telling me about a movie she saw over the weekend. I look down at my sandwich and start pulling it apart to see what's inside. Next, I turn around to see what else is going on in the room.

I **am** | **am not** showing expected behavior in this situation.

My friend will think I **am** | **am not** interested in what she's talking about.

She'll probably feel _____ and will have **good** | **uncomfortable** thoughts about me.

5. I'm at home and my mom is helping me with my homework. I think about what she's saying and nod my head as I listen. I look back and forth between my homework and my mom while she talks.

I **am** | **am not** showing expected behavior in this situation.

My mom will think I **do** | **do not** want her help with my homework.

She'll probably feel _____ and will have **good** | **uncomfortable** thoughts about me.

The Hidden Rules, Expected and Unexpected Behavior: Figuring It All Out!

Hidden rules are clues to the behaviors that are expected in a situation. This is an important idea to keep in mind when you're around other people—even if you're not talking or interacting with them! But sometimes it can be hard to figure out the hidden rules. Thinking with your eyes and being a social detective can help!

As you read the situations below, let's consider the hidden rules. Follow the directions in each to complete the exercise. Take your time—a lot of thinking is going on to figure these out!

SITUATION 1

You enter a room where chess club is happening. Your friend is there and you want to talk to her. You'll need to use your body, eyes, ears, and brain to figure out the hidden rules and know what to do or say.

Put the following thoughts or actions in the correct order by numbering them 1–5.

_____ As you approach your friend, make sure your head, shoulders, arms, and feet are facing her. Stop when you're about one arm's length away.

_____ Notice what your friend is doing and whether she's alone or talking to someone.

_____ Stand where you are for a moment and look for your friend.

_____ Wait for your friend to look at you. Once she does (this tells you she's interested in what you're going to say), you can say something to start the conversation.

_____ If you think it's a good time, walk over slowly to her.

The Hidden Rules, Expected and Unexpected Behavior: Figuring IT ALL OuT!

SITUATION 2

You see some kids you know standing together in a circle at an after school event. You want to join their group. Put these hidden rules related to body, eyes, ears, and brain in the group in the correct order by numbering them starting with 1. Be careful! There are some trick statements and unexpected behaviors mixed in. If you find any, put a line through them.

_____ As you enter the group, keep your head, toes, hips, shoulders, and face turned toward the middle of where the people are standing.

_____ Observe the group and look for clues that this may be a good time to join them. For instance, does everyone seem calm and happy or are people arguing or looking mad? Those are clues!

_____ Wave your arms around and yell to the group, "Here I am! I'm here! I'm here!"

_____ Notice who is talking in the group. Look toward that person, and as different people speak, shift your eyes to keep thinking about the speaker and what he or she is saying. It's okay to look around a little bit, but mostly keep your eyes on the speaker.

_____ After you have approached and entered the group, stand about the same distance as you see others standing to each other.

_____ Try to notice if there's a "hole" or a space between two people where you could enter the group or see if people move a little apart to make room for you to join them.

_____ Just as soon as you're in the group, interrupt the speaker and say, "Hey, what's goin' on?"

_____ Walk up to the group and as you do, see if anyone looks at you.

_____ As you go up to the group find the person you like best and stand right behind that person.

123

The Hidden Rules, Expected and Unexpected Behavior: Figuring IT ALL OuT!

Chapter 7: Thinksheet 8
Page 3 of 3

SITUATION 3

You're on a field trip with your class to a local vegetable farm. The owner of the farm is leading the group to different patches of vegetables. At each one, the group stops, the owner talks about the veggie, how to grow it, its nutritional value, and other interesting facts about it, and then the class moves on to the next patch. Read the following and put an "E" next to the items you think are the hidden rules/expected behaviors in this situation. Put a "U" next to items that might be considered unexpected behaviors in this situation.

_____ Think with your eyes to notice when the group starts to move.

_____ Make a guess about where you think the owner is going next, and then run ahead to that place.

_____ Keep your body moving in the same direction and at the same pace (speed) as the group.

_____ When you have a question, raise your hand and wait for the owner to call on you before speaking.

_____ Sit down in the dirt to look at a vegetable you think is interesting.

_____ Pick one of the vegetables and start eating it.

_____ Listen for clues that indicate the group may be stopping or moving again.

_____ Try not to touch other people, but if it's crowded your body may bump into another person's body.

_____ Don't worry about keeping with the group. As long as you can see the rest of the group, you can go anywhere you want.

_____ Interrupt the owner and talk about the flower garden your mom has in the backyard.

_____ Instead of looking at the owner while he speaks, you stare at one of the other kids in the group.

Chapter 8
Extension Activities &
Thinksheets

Thinking of Others
Versus Just Me

Group MuraL

A collaborative art project or a group mural is a good backdrop to practice the social concepts in this chapter.

1. Have the group decide on a location where many things are going on, such as a zoo, a city, the rainforest, or a playground. You can propose locations for them to discuss.

2. Ask students to each draw a picture of their choice set in that locale. Give the students five to ten minutes to draw, and then collect their drawings.

3. Next ask them to work as a group to make a large drawing of the same setting. You can either hang a big piece of paper on the wall or use one large piece of paper that gets passed around a table. Have the students take turns adding one item at a time to the shared mural.

   As students take turns, talk about the different tasks. For the first drawing they used Just Me thinking because they could do their own thing, and that was fine and expected. But now, during the second activity, they need to be Thinking of Others people. To do this group drawing, each person needs to think about what the previous people have drawn, add related items, and move at a pace that's good for the group (for example, wait their turns to add an item, not take too long on a turn, etc.).

4. The drawing will likely grow and change in unanticipated positive ways. You can use this as an opportunity to reflect on how Thinking of Others actions can be good and fun for everyone. Explain that as we think about each other and what other people have done in our presence, our ideas may grow, change, and become more creative as a result. This helps everyone feel good.

126

Identifying Just Me and Thinking of Others Behaviors

Being a **Just Me** person means you're doing what you want to do and you're not thinking about others. It can be okay to be a Just Me person when what you're doing won't disrupt or bother others. Most of the time that's when you're by yourself.

Being a **Thinking of Others** person means you're thinking about how your behavior makes others think and feel. You're thinking about the people you're sharing space with at the moment or the people who may be coming to share that space very soon.

Let's practice figuring out whether your behavior in a situation is Just Me behavior or Thinking of Others behavior. Read the situations below. For each, decide whether it's a Just Me or a Thinking of Others type of behavior and circle your answer.

1. Mom just got home from grocery shopping and is unloading lots of bags of food from the car. I look up from playing my video game and say, "I'm hungry. What's for dinner?"

   Just Me | **Thinking of Others**

2. After I eat my cereal, I put my bowl in the dishwasher.

   Just Me | **Thinking of Others**

3. I'm watching television. I notice my sister is doing her homework in the next room so I turn down the volume.

   Just Me | **Thinking of Others**

4. I'm in the cafeteria and want to buy lunch. There's a long line of students. I don't feel like waiting so I go to the front of the line.

   Just Me | **Thinking of Others**

5. I'm in the school library with my class. Most kids are reading quietly. I joke and laugh loudly with my friend.

   Just Me | **Thinking of Others**

6. My mom packed chocolate chip cookies in my lunchbox. I know my friend really likes these too, so I offer to share some with her.

   Just Me | **Thinking of Others**

7. I'm at home in my bedroom and my mom and brother are downstairs. I just downloaded some new music and am excited to hear it. I turn the volume up to its loudest level and then hit play.

   Just Me | **Thinking of Others**

8. I'm visiting my grandparents in Arizona and they offer to take me to see the Grand Canyon. I tell them, "Why would I want to see a big hole in the ground?"

   Just Me | **Thinking of Others**

9. I'm walking home after a tough day at school. There's no one around so I sing out loud while I listen to my favorite song on my iPod.

   Just Me | **Thinking of Others**

10. My class is taking a spelling test. I yell out to my teacher when I'm ready for the next word.

    Just Me | **Thinking of Others**

11. When I get home from school, I take off my coat and leave it on the floor.

    Just Me | **Thinking of Others**

12. I'm at home in my room and my dad is outdoors mowing the lawn. I turn up the volume on my speakers while I play my video game to get the full experience.

    Just Me | **Thinking of Others**

How Others Feel About Just Me and Thinking of Others Thinking and Behavior

Read the following situations using your best social thinking abilities. For each, think about whether Just Me or Thinking of Others thinking was used. Also think about how others probably felt in each situation.

 Choose which type of thinking was used and the best feeling word from the list. Circle or underline your answers.

1. It's the beginning of the school day. My class is listening to morning announcements. One student talks loudly to his neighbor while most people are trying to listen. The teacher asks him to be quiet, but he keeps talking.

   He's being a **Just Me** | **Thinking of Others** person.

   Most people in the class probably feel **annoyed** | **content** | **relaxed** | **furious** because they want to hear the announcements.

2. We're taking turns shooting hoops on the schoolyard. I notice a student who is new to our school watching the game from the sidelines. I invite her to join us.

   I'm being a **Just Me** | **Thinking of Others** person.

   The girl probably feels **impatient** | **sad** | **frustrated** | **happy** because she was invited to play.

3. Several of us are working together in class on a group project. Most of us agree on the tasks we'll each do. One student doesn't like what he's supposed to do, and keeps complaining to us all that he'll quit the group if he doesn't get his way.

   This student is being a **Just Me** | **Thinking of Others** person.

   The other kids in the group probably feel **frightened** | **irritated** | **relaxed** | **okay** because we want to get started with the project and can't.

4. My desk at school is a mess with things stacked on top of each other! Every time I try to get one thing out of the pile, a bunch of other things fall to the floor. But I figure it's my desk so it's up to me to decide how neat it is.

   I'm being a **Just Me** | **Thinking of Others** person.

   It's true the desk is mine and I can organize it my way but my teacher and classmates might feel **frustrated** | **content** | **comfortable** | **happy** when they have to look at my mess and avoid tripping over my things.

5. I'm at the grocery store with my mom. I notice she put my favorite snack in the shopping cart!

   My mom is being a **Just Me** | **Thinking of Others** person.

   I feel **excited** | **neutral** | **worried** | **impatient** because I'm looking forward to eating that snack later!

6. My sister is watching TV in the family room by herself. She decides to go upstairs instead. When she leaves the family room, she doesn't turn off the TV. When my mom comes in the room later she turns off the TV and feels **angry** | **bashful** | **eager** | **bothered** because we wasted electricity.

   My sister was being a **Just Me** | **Thinking of Others** person.

7. A student is using the computer at the library and has been using it for a long time! Other kids are waiting to take a turn and are starting to feel **surprised** | **glad** | **shy** | **impatient**

   The student on the computer is being a **Just Me** | **Thinking of Others** person.

Describing JUST Me and Thinking of Others Behavior in Your Own Words

⭐ **Read each situation below. Think of one Just Me response and one Thinking of Others response that someone might have in the situation. Then, describe how each response might make others feel.**

1. I'm busy playing my favorite video game in the family room. My dad comes in and says, "Hi! What are you doing?"

   If I'm thinking like a **Just Me** person, I might: _____

   _____

   This could make my dad feel _____.

   If I'm thinking like a **Thinking of Others** person, I might: _____

   _____

   This could make my dad feel _____.

2. I'm in school and the teacher is reading a book to the class that I've already read. I didn't like it that much when I read it on my own. I like it even less right now!

   If I'm thinking like a **Just Me** person, I might: _____

   _____

   This could make my teacher and classmates feel _____.

   If I'm thinking like a **Thinking of Others** person, I might: _____

   _____

   This could make my teacher and classmates feel _____.

3. We're doing math in class. The problems we're doing are really easy for me. I notice they're hard for some kids though.

   If I'm thinking like a **Just Me** person, I might: _____

   _____

   This could make my teacher and classmates feel _____.

   If I'm thinking like a **Thinking of Others** person, I might: _____

   _____

   This could make my teacher and classmates feel _____.

4. A group of us are on the schoolyard after lunch and we're trying to decide what to do. I want to just hang out and talk but my friends want to play basketball.

   If I'm thinking like a **Just Me** person, I might: _____

   _____

   This could make the other kids feel _____.

   If I'm thinking like a **Thinking of Others** person, I might: _____

   _____

   This could make the other kids feel _____.

5. I'm on a camping trip with my family. We've just arrived and everyone is helping unload the car and set up the tent.

If I'm thinking like a **Just Me** person, I might: _____

_____

This could make my family feel _____.

If I'm thinking like a **Thinking of Others** person, I might: _____

_____

This could make my family feel _____.

6. I'm on a field trip to the science museum with my class. Everyone is taking a break to have a snack but I want to keep moving to get to the astronomy room sooner.

If I'm thinking like a **Just Me** person, I might: _____

_____

This could make my class feel _____.

If I'm thinking like a **Thinking of Others** person, I might: _____

_____

This could make my class feel _____.

Chapter 9
Extension Activities & Thinksheets

How Big Is My Problem?

Problems Come in ALL Sizes

Lesson 4: Problem Solving (page 44) of *Think Social!* is an excellent activity to practice concepts discussed in this chapter. This activity is often successful when presented in a format similar to the suggested activity in Chapter 1.

To start, present the students with a variety of problems and think together about what size they might be: big, medium, or a small problem (a glitch).

1. Write several problems on individual index cards.

2. Give each student a piece of paper and ask students to draw three columns with the headings: big, medium, and glitch.

3. Read a problem out loud, or give it to a student to read out loud.

4. Invite student discussion about the size of the problem. Once a consensus is reached, have the students write the problem in the appropriate column on their sheets. If there are glitches common to the group, be sure to include these as examples!

Identifying The Size of Problems

Problems come in many different sizes. To be a good social thinker I need to learn to identify the size of my problem.

A **BIG** problem is one that causes people we care about to become hurt or sick. Or they can't make money for a while or they lose their place to live. Big problems are serious problems that adults are in charge of. They're too big for kids to figure out what to do.

A **MEDIUM** problem is one that we didn't expect and isn't easy to quickly fix. Medium problems may include fighting with another person, losing something important to you, or someone saying something really mean to another person. Medium problems will make you or someone around you upset. Adults expect kids to help solve medium problems. But it may take a little bit of time for a kid to not be upset about the problem.

A **SMALL** problem, or a **GLITCH**, is a little unexpected problem that can be easily fixed. If you stay calm, stop to think about its size, and remember small problems are really no big deal, glitches can go away pretty quickly. Often glitches just affect you or maybe one other person.

Review the list of problems that follows. Think about whether each is a big problem, a medium problem, or a glitch and put an "X" in that column.

The Situation	BIG Problem	MEDIUM Problem	SMALL Problem/ GLITCH
1. Someone doesn't say hi to me.			
2. I lose a game.			
3. I scrape my knee but it doesn't bleed.			
4. I invite a friend to play and he says no.			
5. My dog dies.			
6. I have to wait for my turn.			
7. My clothes get wet when I wash my hands.			

Identifying The Size of Problems

The Situation	BIG Problem	MEDIUM Problem	SMALL Problem/ GLITCH
8. My house floods after a big storm.			
9. I forget something at school that I wanted to bring home.			
10. I get hurt and need to go to the hospital.			
11. My friend is sick and can't come over to hang out today.			
12. I'm crossing the street and get hit by a person on a bicycle. We both fall and have some scrapes and bruises.			
13. I rip my paper.			
14. My father gets fired from his job.			
15. I don't get to go first.			
16. My doctor gives me a shot in my arm.			
17. My neighbor's house is on fire.			
18. We had a bad storm and our entire city lost its power for five days.			
19. I throw a baseball and it breaks the kitchen window.			
20. My best friend moves away.			
21. Our class has a substitute teacher for one day.			
22. I forget my sneakers and today is gym class.			
23. My tooth aches and I have to go to the dentist.			
24. The girl I have a crush on ignores me.			
25. Our field trip to the science museum is cancelled.			

Why Problems Are Different Sizes

REMEMBER:

Big problems:

- Are serious problems that adults are in charge of

- Are too big for children to figure out what to do

- May be about people getting seriously hurt, very sick, or losing their place to live

Medium problems:

- Aren't easy to quickly fix

- Will make you or someone around you upset

- Are ones that adults expect kids to help solve

Glitches:

- Are little unexpected problems that can be easily fixed as long as you stay calm

- May only affect you or maybe one other person

Pick two problems from each column in Thinksheet #1 and write them below. Explain why each is a big problem, a medium problem, or a glitch.

1. _____

   is a **big problem** because _____

   _____ .

2. _____

   is a **big problem** because _____

   _____ .

Why Problems Are Different Sizes

1. _____

is a **medium problem** because _____

_____ .

2. _____

is a **medium problem** because _____

_____ .

1. _____

is a **small problem/glitch** because _____

_____ .

2. _____

is a **small problem/glitch** because _____

_____ .

140

Thinking About Problem Sizes in My Own Life! Making The Idea of Problem Sizes Real To Me

Problems happen to all of us and all the time! Let's brainstorm, or think together as a group, about different real life problems you've observed, heard about, or experienced in your own lives. These may have happened today, last week, or anytime in the past year or more, to you or other people!

How many *real* problems can you come up with for each size? List them below in the space provided. It's okay if the number of problems for each size is different.

BIG problems we've observed, heard about, or experienced	MEDIUM problems we've observed, heard about, or experienced	SMALL problems, or GLITCHES, we've observed, heard about, or experienced

Thinking About Problem Sizes in My Own Life! Making The Idea of Problem Sizes Real To Me

Now, let's put these ideas together and make some smart guesses.

What size problems were easy to think of? _____

What size problems were harder to think of? _____

Why do you think that is? _____

_____

Now, pick one problem from each column on the previous page and discuss who helped make each problem better, how this was done, and how long it took. Note your answers below.

Problems	Who helped with this problem?	How did they help make it better?	How long did it take?
BIG:			
MEDIUM:			
GLITCH:			

Chapter 10
Extension Activities & Thinksheets

Thinking About My Reaction Size

Try This Reaction on for Size!

For this chapter, you can use any of the problems you discussed with students in the previous activity or use different ones.

1. Act out different reactions to the problems in the activity for Chapter 9. For example, you could pretend to cry and stomp your feet, say things such as, "No big deal" and "It's okay," swipe materials off the table onto the floor, or sigh loudly while rolling your eyes.

2. Invite students to rate the size of your reaction (big, medium, little), and then determine whether it was expected given the problem presented.

Note: The lesson mentioned in Chapter 9 from *Think Social!* applies to this chapter as well. You could also pair this activity with the visual scale found in *The Zones of Regulation* by Leah Kuypers (Think Social Publishing, 2011) Reproducible W, page 126. Students could point to the number on the scale (1–5) they think matches your reaction size. Another useful resource is *The Incredible 5-Point Scale* by Kari Dun Buron and Mitzi Curtis (2003). You can also find a wall poster that explores problems and reaction size at the Social Thinking website, www.socialthinking.com. Search for the product "Size of My Problem Poster."

Give students practice in managing the little glitches that are such a regular part of daily life. It's harder than it seems for our students! After you have role played to ensure understanding of reaction sizes, present the students one at a time with a hypothetical glitch from the situations you used above. Ask them to respond using a small reaction of their choice such as "Oh well," "Maybe next time," "No big deal," or "That's okay."

Identifying The Size of Different Reactions

When we have a problem, we also have a feeling about it, called our "reaction." It's expected behavior that our reaction size matches the size of the problem. For instance, if we have a small problem, we should have a small reaction.

We think with our eyes and use our social thinking to help us match our reaction size to the size of our problem. First let's practice figuring out different sizes of reactions.

Below is a list of possible reactions to a problem. Decide whether the reaction is BIG, MEDIUM, or SMALL and put an "X" in that column.

Reaction to a Problem	BIG Reaction	MEDIUM Reaction	SMALL Reaction
1. Crying out loud or sobbing			
2. Saying, "no big deal"			
3. Staying calm			
4. Throwing an object at another person			
5. Swiping all the pieces off a game board			
6. Taking a deep breath			
7. Saying, "I feel worried about this."			
8. Almost crying			
9. Asking an adult for help			
10. Uncontrollable laughing			

145

Reaction to a Problem	BIG Reaction	MEDIUM Reaction	SMALL Reaction
11. Stomping my feet			
12. Yelling out in class			
13. Saying things that are rude or unfriendly to another person			
14. Saying, "Okay, I understand."			
15. Being really disappointed			
16. Having a tantrum			
17. Saying positive things to myself like, "Everything will be okay."			
18. Hitting or kicking another person			
19. Destroying something that belongs to someone else			
20. Being flexible or being okay with something different than what I was expecting			

Social Thinking and Me

146

My Reactions and Other People

It's expected behavior for my reaction to be only as big as my problem. When my reaction size matches the size of my problem, other people will have okay and sometimes even good thoughts about me. When my reaction is bigger or smaller than the size of my problem, other people may feel tense, annoyed, or nervous. They'll have uncomfortable thoughts about me.

Your reaction size should match the size of your problem.

⭐ **Read the following situations and use your social thinking to identify (1) the size of the problem and (2) the size of the expected reaction. Then make a smart guess about how others might feel. Circle what kind of social thoughts they might have.**

1. My dad says I have to share my favorite set of Legos with my brother and I really don't want to. I say to myself, "No big deal," and let my brother take a turn.

   This problem was **big/medium/small**. My reaction was **big/medium/small**. My dad probably feels _____ and probably has **good** | **okay** | **uncomfortable** thoughts about me.

2. There's a fire down the street. I notice it and yell to my mom, "Help! Help! Call 911!"

   This problem was **big/medium/small**. My reaction was **big/medium/small**. My mom probably has **good** | **okay** | **uncomfortable** thoughts about me and feels _____ about the fire.

My Reactions and Other People

3. I'm playing a game on my tablet and my mom asks me to stop because it's time for lunch. I take a deep breath and remind myself that I can probably play again later.

   This problem was **big/medium/small**. My reaction was **big/medium/small**. My mom probably feels _____ and probably has **good** | **okay** | **uncomfortable** thoughts about me.

4. I'm feeling really cranky and my sister keeps asking me to play. I yell, "Go away and leave me alone forever!"

   This problem was **big/medium/small**. My reaction was **big/medium/small**. My sister probably feels _____ and probably has **good** | **okay** | **uncomfortable** thoughts about me.

5. I want to wear my favorite shirt, but my dad tells me it's in the laundry. Even though I feel disappointed, I decide to wear another shirt instead.

   This problem was **big/medium/small**. My reaction was **big/medium/small**. My dad probably feels _____ and probably has **good** | **okay** | **uncomfortable** thoughts about me.

6. I'm riding my bike and it gets a flat tire. I walk home with my bike and ask my mom for help fixing it.

   This problem was **big/medium/small**. My reaction was **big/medium/small**. My mom probably feels _____ and probably has **good** | **okay** | **uncomfortable** thoughts about me.

7. My friend scratched one of my favorite DVDs by accident. I tell him that I'm going to scratch one of his DVDs.

    This problem was **big/medium/small**. My reaction was **big/medium/small**. My friend probably feels _____ and probably has **good** | **okay** | **uncomfortable** thoughts about me.

8. I'm working in a group with two other classmates. They don't want to do the project the way I want to do it. I get really mad and tell them, "You're both going to pay for this at recess."

    This problem was **big/medium/small**. My reaction was **big/medium/small**. My teacher and classmates probably feel _____ and probably have **good** | **okay** | **uncomfortable** thoughts about me.

9. I answer a question wrong in class. I yell out, "This is stupid!"

    This problem was **big/medium/small**. My reaction was **big/medium/small**. My teacher and classmates probably feel _____ and probably have **good** | **okay** | **uncomfortable** thoughts about me.

10. My teacher is talking and I'm feeling bored. I do my best to look at her and think about what she's saying.

    This problem was **big/medium/small**. My reaction was **big/medium/small**. My teacher and classmates probably feel _____ and probably have **good** | **okay** | **uncomfortable** thoughts about me.

Matching My Reaction To The Size of The Problem

⭐ **Read the following problems and identify their size. Give two possible reactions that match the size of the problem. Remember, when your reactions match the size of the problem, this helps others feel comfortable and have okay thoughts about you.**

1. I feel like I never get to be the line leader at school!

   This problem is **big** | **medium** | **small**.

   Two possible reactions that match the size of this problem are:

   a. _____

   b. _____

2. Look at the picture below. The boy standing on the slide is doing something dangerous. He could get hurt. One of his peers is egging him on (that means: encouraging his behavior) and two of the other kids look worried.

   This problem is **big** | **medium** | **small**.

   Write two possible reactions the peers might have that match the size of this problem:

   a. _____

   b. _____

Matching My Reaction To The Size of The Problem

3. In the picture below, three girls are being unkind and bullying the girl in the pink shirt.

This problem is **big** | **medium** | **small**.

Write two possible reactions the girl in the pink shirt might have that match the size of her problem:

a. _____

b. _____

4. I left my lunch at home and now I don't have anything to eat.

This problem is **big** | **medium** | **small**.

Two possible reactions that match the size of this problem are:

a. _____

b. _____

5. My mom catches me taking money out of her purse.

This problem is **big** | **medium** | **small**.

Two possible reactions that match the size of this problem are:

a. _____

b. _____

6. I accidentally slam my locker on my hand and it's hurting a lot.

This problem is **big** | **medium** | **small**.

Two possible reactions that match the size of this problem are:

a. _____

b. _____

7. I come home from a friend's house and realize one of my earrings is missing.

This problem is **big** | **medium** | **small**.

Two possible reactions that match the size of this problem are:

a. _____

b. _____

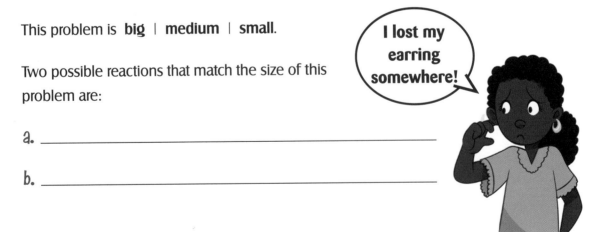

Chapter 11
Extension Activities & Thinksheets

Doing an Activity or Just Hanging Out

Ready... Set... Set Up!

The focus of this activity is centered on game set up and how quickly your students can figure out what needs to be done and then do it. You'll time their efforts and keep a record of how they do.

1. Pick a game your students are familiar with and enjoy playing.

2. Introduce the activity and explain that together you'll be talking about game set up, rather than game play.

3. The objective is for students, as a group, to think about and define all the decisions that must be made as part of game set up. For example, when playing Monopoly, the group needs to decide who uses what game piece, who puts the cards on the board, who is in charge of properties, and who is in charge of the money (the banker). They must also decide who goes first and the general order that students will take turns.

4. Let them know you'll time them to see how quickly they can move through these decisions as a group.

5. The activity starts when you say, "Go." As a group the students need to think about, discuss, and then carry out the decisions/steps in game set up.

6. As needed, you can step in to offer comments or helpful advice if they're overlooking any parts of game set up or if any students are not getting involved in the process.

7. The clock stops when set up is completed and they're ready to play the game.

8. Talk about how the group worked together (or didn't) and whether set up went quickly or whether set up took longer than expected, and why. Help students discover these things on their own by asking leading questions: "Set up took a long time. Can you identify one or two things that caused this?" or "Good job! You went through set up quickly, leaving more time to play together. What did you do as a group to make set up go so smoothly?" Guide them to arrive at the conclusion themselves that the longer set up takes, the less time their group has to play the game.

9. Keep a record of their progress to compare as they go through the activity again with the same game and with different games.

154

10. Students can try to beat their previous set up time on the same game, or arrive at a "best and lowest" time overall.

Variations

- As your students become better at game set up, expand the learning process by starting at the point where the group needs to collectively decide what game to play first, followed by going through the decisions involved in set up. Having the ability to use flexible thinking, be part of the group, and reach consensus are important skills to practice!

- Go through the same activity, this time concentrating on clean up.

- Using the same general activity flow, pick a time when kids are just hanging out instead of their time being focused on a game or activity. Point out that there still is "set up" (where are they going to hang out, for how long, etc.) and "clean up" (saying goodbyes, maybe planning their next time together) although these parts of their time together look a little different.

Identifying The Three Parts of an Activity/Hanging Out

> Although most people don't talk about it, whenever kids (or adults) get together to do something fun together, or just hang out, there are three parts to the activity: set up, doing the activity/hanging out, and clean up. It's expected that each person participates in all three parts of the experience.
>
> When we use flexible social thinking, we can organize ourselves so that set up and clean up go quickly, leaving more time for the fun!

⭐ **For each activity listed, decide which part is set up, which part is doing the activity/ hanging out, and which part is clean up. Draw a line from each part to its corresponding part of play.**

1. **Arts and crafts**

   Set up

   • Make a cool art project — paint, draw, sculpt, bead, etc.

   Doing the activity/ Hanging out

   • Get the needed materials from the art closet and put them on the table.

   Clean up

   • Put the art materials back in their boxes or containers, and put them back in the closet.

2. **Playing Capture the Flag**

   Set up

   • Decide as a group that it's time to end the game.

   Doing the activity/ Hanging out

   • Run around and work with your team to defend and/or capture the flag.

   Clean up

   • Find items to be the "flags," and set up the boundaries of the game using a rope and cones.

3. Checkers

- Take the box off the shelf and take the game board out of the box. Decide who will be what color and put the pieces on the board.

- Put all of the pieces back in the box and put the box back on the shelf.

- Play the game — move pieces, make jumps, and get Kings. Be a good sport during play.

Set up

Doing the activity/
Hanging out

Clean up

4. Basketball

- Pass the ball, shoot the ball, try and stop the other team from getting baskets, and run up and down the court.

- Get a basketball and decide who will be on what team, what position each person will play, and which team shoots into which basket.

- Say "good game" to the other team, maybe shake hands, and put the ball away.

Set up

Doing the activity/
Hanging out

Clean up

5. Hanging out with friends

- Just hang out: talk, laugh, text, etc.

- Get together at the agreed upon time and talk about what to do.

- Talk about another time to get together, say good-byes, leave.

Set up

Doing the activity/
Hanging out

Clean up

When SeT up and CLean up Take Too Long

> Sometimes we have only a certain amount of time to do an activity and usually kids want to spend most of their time in the fun part! When set up or clean up takes too long, other kids start to feel frustrated or annoyed. When everyone works together during set up and clean up, most kids stay happy and relaxed.

To follow are some examples of what set up and clean up could be like. Decide for each situation whether set up or clean up is (a) taking too long or (b) is moving along at an expected pace. Remember, when set up and clean up are moving at an expected pace, everyone feels good. Circle the best answer.

1. I'm getting ready to play a board game with two friends. We can't agree who will go first. We've been arguing about it for a few minutes. In this situation:

   a. Set up is taking too long! We're losing time that we could be playing. People are feeling frustrated!
   b. We're setting up quickly and are almost ready to play! Everyone feels good.

2. I'm playing a video game with one friend. We quickly flip a coin to choose who will go first. In this situation:

   a. Set up is taking too long! We're losing time that we could be playing. People are feeling frustrated!
   b. We're setting up quickly and are almost ready to play! Everyone feels good.

3. I'm building a rocket ship with a friend using cardboard and paint. We argue over whether we should use white or red paint. In this situation:

   a. Set up is taking too long! We're losing time that we could be building the ship. People are feeling frustrated!
   b. We're setting up quickly and are almost ready to build the ship! Everyone feels good.

158

4. We've just finished playing cards. I collect all the cards and hand them to my friend. She puts them in the box and then puts the box away. In this situation:

   a. We're not cleaning up quickly. There's still work to be done. Others are feeling frustrated because they want to do the next thing.

   b. We're working well as a team. We all feel good and are ready to play the next game.

5. We've just finished playing a board game. I lost and want to keep playing until I win. Most kids are ready to do something different. I swipe all the pieces off of the board and they land on the floor. In this situation:

   a. We're not cleaning up quickly. There's still work to be done. Others are feeling frustrated because they want to do the next thing.

   b. We're working well as a team. We all feel good and are ready to play the next game.

6. We've just finished playing tag during lunch period and it's time to come back inside. We move toward the door and get in line quickly. In this situation:

   a. We're not cleaning up quickly. There's still work to be done. Others are feeling frustrated because they want to do the next thing.

   b. We're working well as a team. We all feel good and are ready to do the next thing.

7. My teacher lets us know it's time to work on the school banner we're creating. Four kids in our class are talking by the window rather than helping us get materials. In this situation:

   a. Set up is taking too long! Not all students are helping out. People are feeling frustrated!

   b. Everyone is doing their share of the project.

8. We're at the school library. As I look for a particular book, I take books off the shelf one at a time and put them on the floor. My teacher says it's time to go back to our classroom. I put only a couple of books away. My teacher notices the books I left on the floor and sends me back to put the books away. Everyone has to wait until I'm done. In this situation:

   a. I'm not cleaning up quickly or efficiently. Others feel annoyed with me.

   b. I'm being a good member of the team. I know that if I do things well the first time, it takes less time and everyone will feel okay.

9. Myself and four friends are hanging out on a Saturday afternoon at the skateboarding park. We have an hour to be together. Two of the kids brought their skateboards and want to run the course. The others want to go get a burger instead. We keep going back and forth about what to do for 20 minutes.

   a. Set up is taking too long! People are feeling annoyed!

   b. Everyone is being a flexible thinker so the group can figure out what to do and have fun together.

10. I'm playing a game on our family's tablet with my brother. My dad tells us it's time to put the tablet away and come to dinner. I grab an end of the tablet because I want to have the last turn. We both try to pull it from each other's hands, and nobody gets a last turn.

    a. I'm not cleaning up quickly or efficiently. Others feel annoyed with me.

    b. I'm being a good member of the team as I clean up. I know that if I do things well the first time, it takes less time and everyone will feel happy.

Talking About The Three Parts of Play/Hanging Out in My Own Words

⭐ For the following activities, describe in your own words what set up, doing the activity/hanging out, and clean up would be.

ACTIVITY: PLAYING CATCH DURING RECESS AT SCHOOL

Set up: _____

_____

Activity: _____

_____

Clean up: _____

_____

ACTIVITY: WATCHING A MOVIE WITH A FRIEND

Set up: _____

_____

Activity: _____

_____

Clean up: _____

_____

ACTIVITY: EATING LUNCH WITH A FRIEND

Set up: _____

_____

Activity: _____

_____

Clean up: _____

_____

⭐ Now, for each of these activities, give one example of what might make set up last too long.

1. Set up for playing catch might take too long if _____

_____

2. Set up for watching a movie with a friend might take too long if _____

_____

3. Set up for eating lunch with a friend might take too long if _____

_____

⭐ **List one example of what might make clean up last too long in each situation.**

4. Clean up for playing catch might take too long if _____

   _____

5. Clean up for watching a movie with a friend might take too long if _____

   _____

6. Clean up for eating lunch with a friend might take too long if _____

   _____

⭐ **List three reasons why it's a good idea to move quickly and work cooperatively through set up and clean up when you're with others.**

1. _____

2. _____

3. _____

Helping with or Slowing Down Set up and clean up

⭐ **Take a moment to look at the illustration below about setting up for soccer practice.**

1. Circle the boy or boys who are slowing down set up.

2. Put a check mark next to the boy or boys who are helping set up to go quickly.

3. Make a smart guess about how each boy might be feeling. Write your answers on the numbered lines below the picture.

BOY 1. _____

BOY 2. _____

BOY 3. _____

BOY 4. _____

BOY 5. _____

Helping With or Slowing Down
Set up and Clean up

⭐ **Here's the same situation after the soccer game.**

1. Circle the boy or boys who are slowing down clean up.

2. Put a check mark next to the boy or boys who are helping clean up to go quickly.

3. Make a smart guess about how each boy might be feeling. Write your answers on the numbered lines below the picture.

BOY 1. _____

BOY 2. _____

BOY 3. _____

BOY 4. _____

BOY 5. _____

165

References

Chapter 1: What is Social Thinking?

Briers, S. (2012). *Brilliant Cognitive Behavioral Therapy, 2nd Edition.* Harlow: Pearson Education Limited.

Goleman, D. (2006). *Social Intelligence: The New Science of Human Relationships.* (p. 11). New York: Bantam Books.

Rao, P., Beidel, D., & Murray, M. (2008). Social skills interventions for children with Asperger's syndrome or high-functioning autism: A review and recommendations. *Journal of Autism and Development Disorders, 38,* 353–361.

Wellman, H., & Lagattuta, K. (2000). Developing understandings of mind. In S. Baron-Cohen, H. Tager-Flusberg, & D. Cohen (Eds.), *Understanding other minds: Perspectives from autism and cognitive neuroscience* (pp. 21–49). Second Edition. Oxford: Oxford University Press.

Winner, M.G. (2014). *Why teach Social Thinking: Questioning our assumptions about what it means to teach social skills.* San Jose: Think Social Publishing, Inc.

Chapter 2: Social Thinking = Flexible Thinking

Dawson, P., & Guare, R. (2004). *Executive skills in children and adolescents: A practical guide to assessment and intervention.* New York: Guilford Press.

Happé, F., Booth, R., Charlton, R., & Hughes, C. (2006). Executive function deficits in autism spectrum disorders and attention-deficit/hyperactivity disorder: examining profiles across domains and ages. *Brain and Cognition, 61,* 25–39.

Kenworthy, L., Anthony, L.G., Alexander, K.C., Werner, M.A., Cannon, L., & Greenman, L. (2014). *Solving Executive Function Challenges*. Baltimore: Brookes Publishing Co.

Chapter 3: Social Thinking Vocabulary

Crooke, P.J., Hendrix, R.E., & Rachman, J.Y. (2008). Brief report: measuring the effectiveness of teaching social thinking to children with Asperger syndrome (AS) and high functioning autism (HFA). *Journal of Autism and Developmental Disorders, 38*(3), 581–591.

Marshall, P., & Fox, N. (2006). Biological approaches to the study of social engagement. In P. Marshall & N. Fox (Eds.), *The development of social engagement. Neurobiological Perspectives* (pp. 3–18). New York: Oxford University Press.

Chapter 4: We All Have Feelings

Happé, F., & Williams, D. (2010). Recognising 'social' and 'non-social' emotions in self and others: A study of autism. *Autism: International Journal of Research and Practice, 14*(4), 285–301.

Stallard, P. (2002). *Think Good – Feel Good: A cognitive behaviour therapy workbook for children and young people*. West Sussex: John Wiley & Sons, Ltd.

Chapter 5: Thinking With Your Eyes

Flavell, J. (2004). Theory-of-mind development: Retrospect and prospect. *Merrill-Palmer Quarterly, 50*(3), 274–290.

Jones, E.A, & Carr, E.G. (2004). Joint attention in children with autism: Theory and intervention. *Focus on Autism and Other Developmental Disabilities, 19*(1), 13–26.

Tomasello, M. (1999). Having intentions, understanding intentions, and understanding communicative intentions. In P.D. Zelazo, J.W. Astington, & D.R. Olson (Eds.), *Developing theories of intention: Social understanding and self-control* (pp. 63–75). Mahwah: Lawrence Erlbaum Associates, Inc.

Chapter 6: Thinking about the Hidden Rules and Expected Behavior

Happé, F., & Frith, U. (2006). The weak coherence account: Detail-focused cognitive style in autism spectrum disorders. *Journal of Autism and Developmental Disorders, 36*(1), 5–25.

McLeod, S.A. (2008). *Social Roles*. Retrieved from www.simplypsychology .org/social-roles.html.

Vermeulen, P. (2012). *Autism as context blindness*. Overland Park: AAPC Publishing.

Winner, M.G. (2007). *Social behavior mapping*. San Jose: Think Social Publishing, Inc.

Chapter 7: Keeping My Body, Eyes, Ears, and Brain in the Group

Winner, M.G. (2005). *Think Social! A social thinking curriculum for school-age students*. San Jose: Think Social Publishing, Inc.

Chapter 8: Thinking of Others Versus Just Me

Chandler, M.J. (1973). Egocentrism and antisocial behavior: The assessment and training of social perspective-taking skills. *Developmental Psychology, 9*(3), 326–332, retrieved from http://dx.doi.org/10.1037/h0034974.

Landa, R., & Goldberg, M. (2005). Language, social, and executive functions in high functioning autism. *Journal of Autism and Developmental Disorders, 35*(5), 557–572.

Saulnier, C.A. & Klin, A. (2007). Brief report: Social and communication abilities and disabilities in higher functioning individuals with autism and Asperger syndrome. *Journal of Autism and Developmental Disorders, 37,* 788–793.

Weissbourd, R. (2010, July 22). How do we help children take other perspectives? A conversation with Ellen Galinsky. *Psychology Today,* retrieved from https://www.psychologytoday.com/blog/the-parents-we-mean-be/201007/how-do-we-help-children-take-other-perspectives-conversation.

Chapters 9 & 10: How Big is My Problem? and Thinking About My Reaction Size

Chorpita, B.F., Taylor, A.A, Francis, S.E., Moffitt, C., & Austin, A.A. (2004). Efficacy of modular cognitive behavior therapy for childhood anxiety disorders. *Behavior Therapy, 35,* 263–287.

Lamia, M.C. (2013). *Emotions! Making sense of your feelings.* Washington: American Psychological Association, Magination Press.

Suveg, C., Kendall, P.C., Comer, J., & Robin, J.A. (2006). Emotion-focused cognitive-behavioral therapy for anxious youth: A multiple-baseline evaluation. *Journal of Contemporary Psychotherapy, 36,* 77–85.

Veron, A. (2006). *Thinking, feeling, behaving: An emotional education curriculum for children.* Champaign: Research Press Publishers.

Zeman, J., Shipman, K., & Suveg, C. (2002). Anger and sadness regulation: Predictions to internalizing and externalizing symptomatology in children. *Journal of Clinical Child and Adolescent Psychology, 31,* 393–398.

Chapter 11: Doing an Activity of Just Hanging Out

Winner, M.G. (2005). *Think Social! A social thinking curriculum for school-age students.* San Jose: Think Social Publishing, Inc.

SocialThinking® has so much to offer!

OUR MISSION

At Social Thinking, our mission is to help people develop social competencies to better connect with others and experience deeper well-being. We create unique treatment frameworks and strategies to help individuals develop their social thinking and related social skills to meet their academic, personal and professional social goals. These goals often include sharing space effectively with others, learning to work as part of a team, and developing relationships of all kinds: with family, friends, classmates, co-workers, romantic partners, etc.

ARTICLES

100+ free educational articles and treatment strategies

CONFERENCES, eLEARNING & CUSTOM TRAINING

Courses and embedded training for schools and organizations

PRODUCTS

Books, games, posters, music and more!

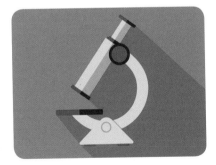

CLINICAL RESEARCH

Measuring the effectiveness of the Social Thinking Methodology

TREATMENT: CHILDREN & ADULTS

Clinical treatment, assessments, school consultations, etc.

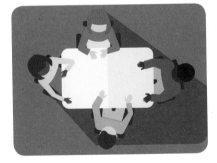

CLINICAL TRAINING PROGRAM

Three-day intensive training for professionals

www.socialthinking.com